The Trouble with Tapioca

The Trouble with Tapioca

Raymond Smit

The Trouble with Tapioca

© Raymond Smit 2013

Published by
Lighthouse Christian Publishing
SAN 257-4330
5531 Dufferin Drive
Savage, Minnesota, 55378
United States of America

www.lighthousechristianpublishing.com

THE TROUBLE WITH TAPIOCA

AN INTRODUCTION:

*"All lies and jest. Still a man hears what he wants to hear
and disregards the rest."*
~ Paul Simon ~

I remember an old story about a man buying a horse. When he looked it over, he was surprised to find it only had three legs.

"That horse is missing a leg," he remarked indignantly.

"No it isn't!" the salesman replied.

"But I can see with my own eyes that it only has three legs!"

"Well, who you gonna believe? Me or your own eyes?"

Lying is nothing new. As long as there have been people, there have been liars. In the beginning Adam and Eve ate forbidden fruit and fibbed about it. God, no fan of prevaricators, kicked them out of His garden. Which just goes to prove that lies are especially hazardous in the hands of beginners.

These days, spin-doctors can stretch the truth further than a Mennonite bending molasses at a taffy pull. Unlike Adam and Eve, today's liars get handsomely paid to do it. So is it any wonder that people have made an art of the lie?

As a member of the fourth estate, I always thought my honesty was above suspicion. But I was wrong. In fact, people often ask me very pointed questions:

"Ray, are your columns true?"

"Do hot dogs contain meat?"

"You're confusing me. What I mean is, are your columns fact or fiction?"

"Yes."

"You often write about your childhood. Are you just making things up or do you have a remarkably good memory?"

"If you tell the truth, you don't need a good memory."

"Say, that's right! Did you just make that up?"

"I forget."

Of course, some people are more pointed than others:

"Hey Ray, are your columns factual or are you just a two-faced, wretched old liar?'

"I'm not old!"

Once, an elderly reader asked me if I'd ever been on stage.

"Why, yes I have," I replied shamelessly.

And that was the honest truth. Unfortunately, I forgot to mention that I had wandered up there during the intermission and when it ended they told me to return to my seat.

With all of that off my chest, I'd like to quote the greatest authority on liars who ever lived: Mark Twain. Twain once wrote about an old rapscallion who showed up for dinner. The fellow spent the entire evening bragging about his remarkable honesty. After twenty minutes, Mark ran to the kitchen to hide the silverware.

Twain also wrote that a historian must 'enlarge the truth by diameters, otherwise his reader would not be able to see it.' It works that way for humour columnists too. The real world needs all the help you can give it to make it funny. As Morey Amsterdam once said, "That's the problem with reality. Not enough punch lines."

Which brings me back to my point. If you can't believe Mark Twain or Morey Amsterdam, then just who can you believe? Politicians? Horse thieves? Me? In essence, the stories in this book are the truth – my truth - or at least my perception of it. Maybe you could think of these tales as parables. That's why most of the names have been changed. Besides, you never know when a process server might be nearby.

Still, I suppose you have the inalienable right to ask me if this book is the truth, the whole truth and nothing but the truth? So let me answer you in a way that will set your mind at rest. When it comes to lying, you can always count on me.

CHAPTER ONE:

BE CAREFUL WHAT YOU WISH FOR

"We would often be sorry if our wishes were gratified."
~ Aesop ~

The Art of the Wheel 'N' Deal

I want to die in my sleep like my grandfather...
Not screaming and yelling like the passengers in his car.
~ Will Shriner ~

My dad was raised poor. When he was sixteen, the world was careening toward the Great Depression. He didn't own a new pair of shoes let alone a car.

My brother Jay and I were raised in the sixties and seventies. When we were teenagers, all we did was dream about cars.

By the time he was forty-five, Dad had overcome his impoverished youth and started a thriving business. There's an old joke that describes to a tee how he felt about his success: A man is hurt in a car accident. The paramedic puts him in the ambulance and asks gently, "Are you comfortable?"

The man replies, "I make a nice living."

Dad bought a new car every two years. But when it came to his sons, he had a decidedly different view. Because, as he always said, "Cars cost money." Of course, with his thick Dutch accent, it sounded more like "Cars coss moe knee."

My brother and I financed our car dreams working in the family business. Sometimes we'd drool over some fancy vehicle in a magazine and Dad would snort, "What ya vant, a Cadillac?" It was the ultimate putdown. Only selfish dilettantes wanted Cadillacs.

One afternoon Jay made an announcement. He had enough money saved to buy a car.

Dad immediately replied, "Cars coss moe knee."

Jay was adamant. He had $800 and he wanted a car - a 'nice' car.

Dad replied, "What ya vant, a Cadillac?"

The next day they went to the car lot. Jay made a beeline for a 1955 Chevy. It was a teenager's dream from the big block engine to the four-speed Hurst shifter. Dad didn't say a word. He seemed more interested in the heavy and slow 1958 Imperial next to it. It was a car only an old lady or a father could love. It should have come with bud vases and doilies. Jay looked at him nervously. I want the Chevy, Dad. It's $800. I don't want the Imperial; it's $1400. Dad nodded. "Leave it to me," he said.
So Jay gave him his $800.

The next day was Jay's birthday. Around four o'clock a white behemoth rolled into the driveway. Jay ran outside staring in disbelief.

"I got you the Imperial, son. I know you really vanted it but it was too expensive for you. So I paid the difference! Happy Birthday!"

As he and Dad took it for a test drive, Jay's friends were pointing and laughing. Dad was smiling beatifically. And Jay? Jay was sniffling and rubbing his eyes.

When they got home, Mom asked, "Does he like it?"

"Like it?" Dad replied. "He was so happy he was practically crying!"

Eventually my turn came. I saved four hundred and fifty dollars and announced that I wanted a sports car.

Dad was not happy: "Cars coss moe knee!"

I insisted.

"All right then give me the moe knee, I get you a car."

Jay violently shook his head no. Dad gave him a look. "You have a migraine?"

A few days later, Dad burst into the house.

"Boy, have I found you a car!"

"Great, what is it?"

"A Volkswagen."

"But I don't like Volkswagens. I want something fast!"

"What you vant, a Cadillac?"

Dad sent me outside. It was a Volkswagen all right. And what a Volkswagen! It had been customized to look like a German army helmet on wheels. The only thing missing was the 'Iron Cross.'

Jay rolled up in his Camaro.

"How much did you pay for it Dad?" Jay asked, biting his lip to keep from laughing.

"I talked him down to $450."

"But I don't like Volkswagens," I asserted, although no one was listening.

"Those Germans are the world's best engineers. Germans are very smart."

"Yeah," Jay replied dryly. "Look how they won those two world wars and all."

Dad gave him a dirty look.

Jay checked out the car and discovered it needed a clutch, brakes and a transmission.

"I'll take care of it," Dad replied.

The next night Dad proudly handed me a cheque. I sold that lemon you bought."

"I bought? How much did I get?"

"Two hundred and fifty dollars."

"I lost two hundred dollars in two days?"

"Cars coss moe knee!"

I had to admit he was right.

A few months later, Jay found me an old 6-cylinder Pontiac sedan for $300. Jay explained that it burned oil and the gas gauge was broken. I didn't mind. Every time I pulled into the Shell station, I chortled, "Fill the oil and check the gas!" Surprisingly, Dad approved of the Pontiac. Looking back I think he would have made a pretty good chess player.

Nowadays I still drive a Pontiac. The paint is dull and the engine's a little tired, but I don't care. I'm not about to buy a new one because "Cars coss moe knee." And when people ask me why I'm driving such an obvious rattle trap, I reply, "What you vant, a Cadillac?"

Dad would be proud.

Confessions of a Reformed Blabbermouth

"When you want to fool the world, tell the truth.
~ Otto Von Bismarck ~

I was never good at keeping secrets when I was young. In fact, I was a blabbermouth. As my brother used to say, "Telephone, telegraph or tell Ray." Of course, nowadays I'm the very soul of discretion.

When I was nine, we bought a new house. Mom's friend Freda said, "You can't have your photography business in that neighbourhood. There's a zoning by-law prohibiting home-based businesses."

Mom immediately started to worry. "What if the by-law officers shut us down?"

Dad replied, "They won't unless some blabbermouth spills the beans!" Curiously, it was that very night that Mom and Dad sat me down for a talk:

"Ray, we need you to keep a secret. You can't tell anyone we have a business in the house because the by-law officers will shut it down. This is very, very important! Our livelihood depends on it!" It all seemed very confusing and scary to a nine-year-old. But I swore I wouldn't tell anyone that Dad was a photographer.

The next day I met some of the neighbourhood children: "What does your Dad do?"

I felt a surge of panic. If I told them he was a photographer, we'd lose the house, Mom would go on trial and the bilateral officers would shoot my dog. In sheer desperation I blurted out, "My father's a war hero. He won the Victoria Cross." Dad did have a box of medals in the basement, but they were for good conduct.

One of the boys replied, "Isn't your father Dutch? How can he have an English medal?"

"He's bilingual."

"That's stupid. No foreigner has ever won the Victoria Cross!"

"Not the Victoria Cross," I replied cleverly. "It's the Vancouver Cross!"

Of course, adults aren't usually as gullible as children are. A few days later one of the neighbours stopped by. "It's a great honour to meet you Mr. Smit."

"It is?"

"Yes, it's not often a man of your distinction graces our presence."

"I just move in and you vant to give me presents?"

"My children tell me you're a war hero."

"Vell, I did my part."

"You have an odd accent. What part of Britain are you from?"

"Amsterdam."

"If you're Dutch how on earth did you get the Victoria Cross?"

"Cross? I'm not even Catholic."

Later that night Dad had a talk with me. "Why did you tell the neighbours that I won the Victoria Cross?"

"So the bisexual officers don't send Mom to prison!"

The next day I obediently told my new friends that Dad wasn't really a war hero.

"What does he do then?"

I got a sudden flash of inspiration. "He's a secret agent."

"Oh yeah? Then what's his number?"

"Double Oh Fifty-seven!" He was actually fifty-three but fifty-seven sounded cooler. The kids were intrigued.

"Does his car shoot bullets out of the tailpipe?"

"Uh – sure."

"Can he launch torpedoes from the cigarette lighter?"

"When he's not lighting a cigar."

"Wow. All our stupid car has is power brakes."

That night Mom and Dad and I had another talk. "Have you been telling people your father is a secret agent?"

"Yes Ma'am."

"I thought we told you not to make up stories."

"No Ma'am. You told me not to say Dad was a war hero."

"You should never tell a lie, Ray."

"But you told me not to tell anyone he was a photographer! You told me it was a secret!"

"We didn't tell you to lie. We just told you not to tell the truth!" There was a long silence. Dad and Mom looked at each other. "Go out and play and from now on just tell the whole truth secrets and all!"

"Can I tell how old you are, Mom?"

Mom shook her head and sighed. "Just go out and play!" Sometimes adults are impossible to understand.

I headed outside. "Guys. I have to tell you the truth. My Dad's not a secret agent. He's a photographer. Every baby born in Toronto has their picture taken by my dad's company."

"No way. There's a gazillion babies born every day. How could he take that many pictures?"

"He doesn't. The nurses do it. Then he develops the photos at home."

One of the kids interjected, "Hey maybe the stork takes their pictures before delivering them to the hospital!" Everybody started laughing. "Boy, you've told us some whoppers, Ray, but this one takes the cake!"

I guess OttoVon Bismarck was right. "When you want to fool the world, tell the truth."

In the end, Dad called the zoning department. They said a home business was completely legal. I overheard Dad say that Mom's friend Freda "should keep her big yap shut!" But you won't hear it from me. I'm no blabbermouth.

The Why Chromosome

"She's the kind of girl you want so much it makes you sorry, still you don't regret a single day."
~ John Lennon ~

In the great pantheon of existence there are wildebeests and there are lions. It's a simple matter of genetics.

In my teens, my lack of prowess with women was already legendary, but from the moment I met Jane, I desperately wanted her to be my one and only. Jane was the smartest girl at Sutton District High. She was at the top of her class in every subject and a whole lot better looking than me to boot. She was the stereotypically cute girl next door. I was the boy whose parents keep the shades drawn. Still, miracles happen and quite surprisingly, she agreed to go out with me.

Wanting to prove myself worthy of my ladylove, I tried valiantly to keep up with her in all aspects of life - especially academically. I remember once spending a whole weekend working on a chemistry assignment. Jane did hers between episodes of *Love Boat* and *Fantasy Island*. But all my hard work paid off. I got an A. After class I asked Jane what she got.

"An A plus," she replied nonchalantly.

Life isn't fair.

If I couldn't be as smart as Jane, I thought I should at least be as good looking. So I spent endless hours in front of the mirror trying to look like Don Juan. The closest I ever came was Don Knotts. After all, I was a skinny kid with incredible acne. The day her father met me, he bought 500 shares of Clearasil. Or at least he should have.

Not as smart or attractive as Jane, I set my hopes on my superior athletic ability. One Saturday morning Jane suggested we go bowling.

"Bowling?" I asked suspiciously.

"I've been once or twice. I'm not very good. But it's fun!"

"Okay, let's go," I replied. Score one for the male ego. Sure I'd go bowling. And then once and for all there would be a triumphant resolution to the battle of the sexes.

We warmed up with a few practice frames and Jane threw three straight gutter balls. I was delighted. We were about to start when Jane's friend Jack, the owner, asked if he could roll a game with us.

"Sure," I replied, "if you don't mind bowling with Jane. She's a beginner."

"Okay." he replied with a grin. "Loser buys lunch and Jane gets a 50 pin head start."

Jane stepped up for the first frame and threw a strike.

"Good for you, Jane," I said patronizingly.

Then she threw another one.

"Way to go, Honey."

And then she threw another. And another. And another. As Tom Cruise said in *The Color of Money*, "It's like a nightmare isn't it? It just gets worse and worse."

I'd been hustled.

Jane ended up bowling a 215. Jack threw a 160. And me? I bowled a 45. That's when I realized why men have Y-chromosomes. Because we're always wondering why women are better at everything than us.

Despite the inexorable nature of Jane's victories, I kept searching for something – anything - that I was better at. And I finally did: humour. She might be smarter, better looking and more athletic, but I was funnier.

One night on the way home from a concert, I decided to tell a few jokes at Jane's expense. Truth be told, I was showing off for my brother. Jane was a good sport but her patience was wearing thin. Still, I pressed my luck.

"I'd like to have a battle of wits with you, Jane," I said smugly as she did a slow burn. I was about to deliver the crushing comic blow when she beat me to the punch line.

"No thanks, Ray. It's not sporting to go to war with an unarmed man."

My brother laughed so hard he nearly drove off the road. And I, the supposed sultan of satire, sat stunned and stupefied. As *Mutual of Omaha's* Marlin Perkins might have said, "We see the poor wildebeest struggling in the mud as the lioness moves in for the kill."

I never did find anything I was better at than Jane. We broke up after high school and she eventually married someone better. I wasn't surprised. After all, it's a simple matter of genetics.

DOUBLE BED ENVY

"As innocent as a new-laid egg."
~ W.S. Gilbert ~

Dr. Penelope Leach is a noted psychologist and expert in developmental studies. Dr. Leach has written several books and believes that "guilt is the most destructive of all emotions."

When I was six my Mom and Dad bought an old wreck of a cottage near Lake Simcoe. It was the kind of place that realtors euphemistically refer to as a 'fixer-upper' and lucid people call a 'dump.' It wasn't much but we kids were thrilled. We especially liked the plywood addition at the front, which my eleven-year-old brother dubbed the 'caboose.'

There were two beds in the caboose. One was a surprisingly comfortable double bed. The other was a roll-a-way with a mattress thinner than a humour columnist's wallet. Naturally, Jay and I both wanted the double bed. And so when it came time for our first sleepover a fight broke out that would shame Mike Tyson and Lennox Lewis.

Mom told us that all good children should learn to share. Mothers always say infuriating things like that. Mom decided that Jay would get the double bed for the first week of our vacation and I would get it the second. I was unimpressed by Mom's Solomon-like wisdom until I saw Dad taking off his belt. Suddenly she made all kinds of sense. And when Jay called dibs on the flashlight, I decided to be big about it and offer my consent. After all I didn't want Dad's pants to fall down

After a long week of double bed envy it was finally time to switch sides. Surprisingly, Jay seemed quite happy to let me have the double bed and the flashlight. In fact, after Mom and Dad said good night Jay began to laugh.

"Heh, heh, heh," he intoned somewhat ominously.

"What?" I asked.

"Heh, heh, heh. You'll find out!" he replied sounding for all the world like a young Dracula.

"Find out what?" I gulped.

"Well, I didn't want to tell you this before. Because I hoped the monster would go away," he replied forbiddingly.

"The monster?"

"Yes the monster who lives under the double bed. Heh, heh, heh."

It was uncanny how he made his voice sound just like Bela Lugosi. And his ironic little laugh was beginning to unnerve me.

"Dad says there aren't any monsters."

"The monster made him say that! Heh, heh, heh!"

"Mom!"

"Shh. Be quiet. You don't want the monster to get Mom do you?"

"No…"

"Besides, I'm the only one who knows how to stop the monster. I learned how in Boy Scouts."

"You're not a Boy Scout."

"I'm a secret member. Do you know the Boy Scout motto?"

"Be prepared?"

"Yes. But you don't know the second part. Only Secret Scouts know the second part: 'Always be prepared...for monsters!' Oooooooohhhh. Heh, heh, heh."

"Mom!"

"Shh!"

"I wanna sleep in the other bed!"

"I don't know, Ray. He's a mean monster."

"Please?"

"Okay, okay. But I'll be up all night protecting you so I'll need the flashlight and you'll have to lend me your new comic book. Okay?"

"Okay."

"Oh yes and your bubble gum cards."

"Okay."

"Oh, and your yo-yo. Okay?"

"Okay."

"Heh, heh, heh!"

Mom and Dad seemed surprised that I was sleeping on the rollaway the next morning but delighted at my sudden interest in joining the Boy Scouts.

I remember that night very well. So does my brother. I remind him of it often. He feels guilty that he took advantage of me. As I write this he's standing outside in a cold rain trying to fix my car. The water keeps running off the edge of the hood and down his neck. Which brings me back to Dr. Penelope Leach who said, "Guilt is the most destructive of all emotions." She may have a doctorate, but I bet even Dr. Leach doesn't know everything about guilt...or brothers.

"Heh, heh, heh."

The Big Five-Oh No!

"Nostalgia is like a grammar lesson: you find the present tense, but the past perfect!"

~ Owens Lee Pomeroy ~

Turning fifty is like accidentally walking around with your fly open. You hope nobody notices…but they always do!

I guess I worry too much about aging. Especially considering how youthful I am. I was explaining that to my brother the other day as I gazed in the mirror:

"It's amazing, despite my age I still don't look a day over 35."

"Say what?"

"No seriously, I haven't got one wrinkle," I enthused.

"I don't think you have 'one' wrinkle either," Jay retorted mockingly.

"You may jest, but I'm practically a kid."

"You're fifty!"

"I am not! I'm forty-something."

"Well then you've been forty-something for over a decade. For Pete's sake you were born in 19…"

"Never mind, I know when I was born."

Jay shook his head. "Look Ray, now that you're older, why don't you stop worrying about superficial things and start developing your intellect?"

"Well, I did watch PBS the other day."

"That's a good start. What were you watching?"

"The Teletubbies…"

A few weeks later I visited again.

"You know, Jay, I've given some thought to what you said and I've been devoting myself to the intellectual arts.

"Oh, really? How many books a week are you reading?" he asked suspiciously.

"Seven."

"Not including comic books."

"Less than seven."

"You don't read at all, do you?"

"I do too."

"Excluding closed captioning."

"Shut up!"

To my mind there are four sure signs of turning fifty: The first one is memory loss. Of course that doesn't worry me. Because, I'm not fifty. By the way, I should remember to mention that there are four sure signs of turning fifty. And the first one is memory loss.

Another certain sign of turning the half-century is the 'droopies.' A nurse recently told me that once a woman hits the big five-oh everything starts to sag. It's pretty much the same for men. When guys turn fifty instead of a sexy six-pack - they get a noticeable butt crack. (Gentleman, buy some suspenders please!) Instead of pecs, they get specs. And instead of having awesome glutes, they stay at home and dye their roots. Ah, Grecian Formula. Thank goodness I don't need it. I'm not fifty.

The third sign someone has turned the big five-oh is nostalgia. When people reach the half-century they seem to think that everything old is great and everything new is lousy. Well, I'm not like that. I love all the new singers: Mick Jagger, James Taylor and Petula Clark. And I'm not stuck in past. My house has the latest electronics gadgets including a VCR, basic cable and a telephone answering machine. And as for disparaging the present, nothing could be further from the truth. When I was young we had the Beatles, Carly Simon, and long johns. Now they have Rappers, teenage divas and V-thongs. You can choose what you like. But I'm voting for my comfortable cotton briefs.

The fourth and final sign of turning fifty is hair loss. Fortunately, my pompadour is just as thick as ever. Although the last time I got my summer brush cut I couldn't go out without a hat. Apparently the glare was bothering people. Astigmatism, I guess. Coincidentally, when my brother saw my new brush cut he offered me a forty-watt bulb.

"What do you want me to do with that?" I asked warily.

"Stick in your mouth and see if it lights up. You look like Uncle Fester."

Of course, the joke was on him. I couldn't possibly look like Uncle Fester. He was fifty.

All of this brings me back to my original point. Turning fifty is like accidentally walking around with your fly open. The next time I do - or you catch me lying about my age - just tell me to zip it.

And for the record, I'm not fifty!

I'm forty-ten...and holding.

CHAPTER TWO:

THE SECRETIONS OF MY SUCCESS

"Behind every successful man there is a surprised woman."

~ Maryon Pearson ~

Sic Transit Gloria: Or How I Taught Jim Carrey Everything He Knows

"It isn't necessary to be rich and famous to be happy. It's only necessary to be rich."

~ Alan Alda ~

Early on in life my goal was to be famous. That way people would make a big fuss over me and ask for my autograph.

When I was nine, I wanted to be a lead singer like Mick Jagger. Mom was very encouraging. In order to help me get just the right acoustics she'd put me in the recreation room at the far end of the house and close the door. The dog, always amiable, would sing along. The more I sang, the louder she got. When we reached a fever pitch, the neighbours would drop by. I often overheard them mentioning 'animal cruelty' and 'noise pollution.' Mom said it was nice of them to suggest such groovy names for my band.

Strangely, Mom and Dad decided a singing career wasn't my destiny. But they did eventually buy me an acoustic guitar. Dad was adamant that it not be an electric because those awful, longhaired Beatles played electric guitars. I guess he was into Dylan…

After my first lesson, the teacher decided I should play left-handed. I went home and told Dad that I was going to play just like Paul McCartney.

"Paul who?"

"You know, like the Beatles."

"Oh no," he said. "No Beatles. You tell Paul McCartney to find another student."

"But Dad, Paul McCartney wouldn't have come here anyway."

"Unreliable hippies! Talk about lazy. Won't even give lessons at home! All that hair. Terrible! No, you'll take lessons at the conservatory instead."

So, while my friends were forming groups and playing *Hey Jude* and *Jumping Jack Flash,* I was learning the *Pollywog Song* and *The Little Rabbit Dance.* Despite scores of auditions, I wasn't asked to join any rock bands. Professional jealousy I suppose because no one can rock *Miss Holly Had A Dolly* like me.

A few years later, my friend Steve taught me a few simple Chuck Berry tunes. We joined the Sutton high school band and often played concerts at elementary schools from Jackson's Point to Keswick. Having the biggest mouth, I got to emcee. Whenever we did *Johnny*

B Goode, I'd ask, "Do you kids remember the fifties?"

And they'd all scream, "Yeah!"

Then I'd reply, "What a bunch of liars!" Because every one of those kids was born in the sixties. That always got a big laugh. Then I'd tell a few more jokes and we'd play some rock'n'roll.

Years later I learned that Jim Carrey lived in Jackson's Point at exactly that time. Undoubtedly, he was in the audience for some if not all of my performances. Now I don't mean to brag, but he must have been so impressed by my jokes that it inspired him to become a comedian. Yes, in all humility, it was my humour that started Jim Carrey on the road to stardom! Without me he might have ended up as a Port Perry proctologist.

Anyway, after those shows the kids would rush the stage and ask their favourite performers for autographs. So it's very likely I signed an autograph for Jim Carrey. He must have been thrilled!

My quest for fame got sidetracked after high school but was resurrected when I got a newspaper column in 1999. One of the nicer benefits is that, every now and then, someone will write a letter to the editor praising one of my columns. Feeling particularly self-satisfied one afternoon, I asked my brother if he thought people would start asking me for my autograph too.

"Only if it's on a credit card receipt."

"Very funny."

"Look, Ray, how long has it been since someone asked for your autograph?"

"Thirty odd years. So what?"

"So this! *Sic Transit Gloria*. Fame is fleeting."

I guess Jay was right. Fame doesn't last. And I can live with that. After all, I'm a very modest kind of guy. I also take some solace that my protégé Jim Carrey has had some success too. And I'm sure that whenever someone asks for his autograph, he thinks of me. And I guess that's reward enough. So maybe the next time you feel an irresistible urge to ask for my autograph, you should try to contain yourself. Modesty forbids.

Confessions of a Hyper Hypochondriac

"Health nuts are going to feel stupid someday, lying in hospitals dying of nothing."
~ Redd Foxx ~

They say that confession is good for the soul. So I've decided to come clean. I'm a hypochondriac.

So, do I feel better getting that off my chest? Not really. Just because you're a hypochondriac doesn't mean you're not really sick! And having a whole shelf of medical books doesn't prove I'm neurotic either. It just shows I'm cautious and well informed. I may have the lowest cholesterol my doctor has ever seen, but that doesn't ensure I won't have a heart attack any second. Tests can be wrong! And even my kindly doctor won't repeat the same tests over and over and over again.

I was worrying about cholesterol the other day as I waited for my appointment at the Well Street Clinic. I was leafing through a James Thurber novel when it suddenly occurred to me that all my health troubles would be solved if I were a doctor myself. That way I could order any test I wanted, anytime I wanted. As the sun streamed in through the waiting room window I closed my eyes and imagined how it would be:

I was in the lounge at New York Regional General Hospital when a nurse suddenly burst in. "Dr. Smit, we need you in ER stat!" I dropped my Walter Mitty novel and made a wild dash for the doors, my stethoscope gleaming in the reflected admiration of my awestruck colleagues.

A beautiful young woman was laid out on a gurney. She was pale, her trembling crimson lips delineating her exquisite face. I checked her chart and ordered a Chem7 and a BLT.

"Let me see here. A. Thropic. What's your first name dear?"

"Anne."

"Yes, here it is. Miss Anne Thropic. I want you to feel at ease, Anne."

"Are all doctors as good looking as you?"

"Only at the Well street clinic. In fact, I think it's a career prerequisite."

"Is that where you practice?"

"No, I just spend all my free time there."

"Can you help me, Dr. Smit?"

Although I could tell it was dire, I was reassuring. "There, there, my dear. It may be a simple neuropathic artery or a enervating pustule." I grabbed a ball peen hammer and checked her reflexes.

Suddenly an intern, Dr. Henry Honey, cried out, "Dr. Smit, what will we do? Her lips have become unctuous!"

"Get hold of yourself, Honey," I answered brusquely. "I don't tolerate panic in my ER."

"But what if she begins to osculate?"

I repeatedly slapped his face to settle him down.

"Stop it, Honey. Can't you see she's photogenic?"

He began to cry.

"Stop blubbering, man! Worrying won't help her."

"I'm not crying because I'm worried."

"Why then?"

"You've been slapping me with the ball peen hammer."

"Oh…well, let that be a lesson to you. Keep your mind on your work."

I coolly appraised the situation. "Nurse, get me some sorbitol, stat."

"Yes doctor," the nurse curtsied elaborately and ran from the room.

I whispered, "Hold on Julie, I'm going to pull you through. Prepare her for surgery."

We arrived at the O.R. just as Dr. Maxwell Edison, the chief of surgery, rushed in.

"Oh great merciful heavens," he shrieked. "It's paronomasia I've seen cases in Liverpool. She's only got a 1% chance!"

"Get hold of yourself man," I yelled smacking Dr. Honey again with the ball peen hammer. "We can pull her through."

"Yes, of course," Edison replied. "By the way, that's my hammer. Pure silver, you know.

"Honey, be a good lad and return Maxwell's silver hammer."

"Yes, sir."

The scrub nurse dropped her mop and cried out, "The Capresso machine is broken!"

"Calm down," I ordered as I welded the ends together

with a match and some hair gel. "That'll give me enough time to save her."

I took the scalpel and made a lateral incision in her daucus carota. It was a complicated procedure but a few hours later she came to. The operation was a complete success!

One of the nurses gushed, "Doctor Smit, you'll win the Geller Prize for this. Yes and the Buffay, the Tribbiani, the Green and the Bing."

"Now, now. Even though my paronomasia operation will end disease as we know it, I'm just a humble doctor. It's not about prizes or my new Mercedes or my oceanfront home in the Hamptons. It's about the common people I save every day. Like Susan here."

"My name is Anne."

"Whatever."

The nurse began calling. "Dr. Smit, it's time for your Nobel Prize. Ray, it's time."

"Hmmm?"

"Ray it's time!" It was Heidi from the Well street office staff.

"I'd like to thank the Nobel committee."

"Excuse me?"

"I mean, thank you, Heidi."

As I sat in the exam room, I decided not to tell my doctor I had paronomasia. Comprehensive tests would reveal it in due course. Instead, I would persevere - nobly and courageously until the bitter end. And my epitaph?

No doubt it will read, 'Just because you're a hypochondriac doesn't mean you're not really sick.'

Dedicated to the late, great James Thurber

Realtor Ray

"Whoever exalts himself will be humbled."
Matthew 23:12

When I finished school, I discovered that jobs in the social work field were scarce. So I signed on as a realtor while I waited. After all, with a psychology degree, I'd be a lead-pipe cinch to be a successful salesman...

On my first day an experienced realtor named Deke said, "Ray, you need a good start. So I'm going to help you out by giving you one of my listings."

"Gee, thanks, Deke!"

"It's a small lot on the 14th concession near Norwood."

Deke was a swell guy! I wasn't sure where Norwood was but I was happy to have a listing. The next day the owner called.

"This is Mr. Williams. When are you gonna put a sign on my lot?"

"I'll come right now. How's that for service?"

"You should have been here yesterday!"

Sixty miles later I finally found the lot: a swampy overpriced piece of farmland. As I pushed my sign into the muddy ground I was beginning to smell a rat – or was that manure?

The next day the owner called me again.

"We had a storm last night and the sign tipped over."

"Did you put it back up? You live next door."

"That's your job not mine!"

It turned out that Mr. Williams was so obnoxious not one realtor in town was daft enough to work with him. Except, of course, for 'Mr. Psychology Degree.' Nevertheless, I had learned my first lesson: beware of Dekes bearing gifts.

A few days later a young couple called me about a vacant fixer-upper forty miles from Peterborough. I called the listing agent and we were on our way. An hour later we walked up to the front door only to discover that I had forgotten the key. The client's wife noticed an open window at the back of the house. Her irritated husband insisted I climb in. It was a small opening but I was game. Unfortunately, though I was thin as a rail, nature had given me a rather prominent caboose. I was halfway through when I got stuck. It suddenly became very quiet.

"Hey you," someone demanded in a curt voice. " What do you think you're doing?"

"It's okay," I replied. "I'm the realtor."

"I'm the neighbour. Do you have a card?"

A card? I was stuck in a window with my backside hanging out and he wanted a card?

"Could you give me a little help first?"

He gave me a quick, hard push and I sailed through the window to the floor below. Luckily some broken glass and an old table leg broke my fall. When I hobbled outside, the husband announced, "We don't need to see the inside. We hate the neighbourhood."

And that was my second lesson: When you're up to your butt in trouble, don't ask for a push.

The next morning a prosperous-looking older couple came in. They wanted to view waterfront homes. As they piled into the car, I ran back for my briefcase. The office secretary asked me, "Did you qualify those people?"

Qualify them? Me? Who'd be a better judge of people: a realtor with a psychology degree or a secretary?

"I think they're okay," I replied loftily.

We'd already seen several homes when they insisted we stop for lunch. I had a sandwich. They ordered steaks. When the bill arrived, they sat on their hands. Guess which genius got stuck with the bill?

When we got back, I asked them if they'd like to make an offer.

"No. We won't be buying for at least five years. But thanks for the wonderful day!"

The secretary started giggling. I said nothing as I watched them drive off in an old jalopy. And that was my third and final lesson: "'Tis better to be silent and be thought a fool, than to speak and remove all doubt." Apparently even Mark Twain would have made a better realtor than me.

Shortly thereafter, the office manager suggested that I consider another line of work. I got a job at a psychiatric group home. It paid minimum wage but I was happy to get it.

"Whoever exalts himself will be humbled."

Exactly.

THE VELVET FROG

*"If only the talented birds could sing, what a silent world
this would be."*
~ Author unknown ~

As I've mentioned before, I'm not a professional singer, but I always wanted to be one. There are two cardinal sins for singers: warbling out of tune and dismembering the lyrics. Luckily I have reasonable good pitch – just ask the dog – but I do tend to confuse the lyrics:

I remember Christmas Eve when I was ten. The whole family was gathered around the tree when someone suggested I sing, *"Walking In A Winter Wonderland."* I happily obliged:

"Later on, we'll perspire
As we sit by the fire
We're happy tonight
So go fly a kite
Walking in the winter wonderland."

This led to hoots of laughter from the entire family. I was puzzled at the time but now I realize my error. The line is actually, "walking in 'a' winter wonderland not walking in 'the' winter wonderland." Still, why so much hilarity over one little word?

I also remember another time when I sang a stirring version of *"The Christmas Song."*

"Chestnuts roasting on an open fire
Jack's dog licking at your toes
You'll find Carol being hugged by a choir
With great drops dripping from her nose
Everybody knows the turkey had a missing toe
We caught it 'cause it wasn't very bright
Though it's been said many times, many ways
Merry Christmas and good night."

I have to admit that's not exactly the way Mel Torme performed it. For the sake of accuracy I'm pretty sure Mel sang, "Jack's dog licking at your 'nose.'" But that's no reason to snicker at a ten-year-old!

The folks were especially giddy at my rendition of *White Christmas*:

"I'm dreaming of a white Christmas
Just like the ones in Mimico
Where the eaves troughs glisten
And children listen
To hear police cars on the road…

I'm dreaming of a white Christmas
With every Christmas card I write
May your eyes be bleary tonight
And may all your Christmases be white."

Mimico, by the way, is a suburb of Toronto. As I explained to my Mom and Dad at the time, Bing Crosby must have spent a Christmas there. That's why he wrote *"White Christmas"* about it later when he was visiting his pal Irving in Berlin. But that, of course, is common knowledge.

I guess I'll never really understand my family's peculiar reaction to my holiday oratorios. But it's reassuring to know that I've always had a wonderful singing voice and that no matter what, the dog was always ready to harmonize! My father called it morose caterwauling. A morose is a kind of flower, and caterwauling is a Dutch word for the joyful noise that dogs make when they sing along. At least that's what Mom told me. And she should know, she's Dutch.

This Christmas I plan to sing all the parts to *The Nutcracker*. And if one thing is certain, it's that I'll be doing my fair share of morose caterwauling this year. Now where did the dog bury my pitch pipe?

Will I Grow Accustomed To Her Face?

"One of the keys to happiness is a bad memory."
~ Rita Mae Brown ~

All of us are defined by our idiosyncrasies. I have two - my failure to recognize faces and my inability to remember names.

Unfortunately those character flaws ruined my childhood dream of becoming a detective. Why? Because even the smallest change in a criminal's appearance would have left me flummoxed. "I'm sorry sir, the suspect we brought in for questioning had a hat on. You don't. So let me just apologize and unlock these handcuffs for you."

Even mundane changes confuse me. If someone cuts their hair, I'll walk right past them. Which reminds me of a story. A man decided to shave for the first time in twenty years. After the deed was done, he resolved to surprise his family. So he slipped outside and knocked on the front door. When his six-year old daughter opened it he somberly asked, "Excuse me little girl, is your mother home?"

The little girl ran to the kitchen screaming, "Mommy, Mommy, come quick! Daddy shaved off his beard and now he can't remember who he is!"

I can relate. My Dad shaved off his mustache when I was six. I immediately stopped speaking to him. I had to. Mom told me never to talk to strangers.

My problems haven't improved with age. For instance there was my prom. A bunch of us were meeting at my girlfriend Jane's house. Her mother, Mrs. Rousseau, let me in and told me to wait in the living room with the rest of the partygoers.

Apparently Jane was still getting ready so I took a seat. As I looked around the room I saw a vision. She was an angel wearing a chic formal accentuated by gold earrings and an elegant short upswept hairdo. I wondered which one of my lucky friends had scored a date with such an amazing beauty. And though I loved Jane with all my heart, it seemed only polite to introduce myself. I ran the words over in my mind: "Hi. We haven't met yet but I'm Jane's boyfriend, Ray. And you are?"

I was about to take the plunge, when Jane's mom unexpectedly returned to the living room. "Aren't you going to give Jane her corsage?"

"Yes, of course," I answered, wondering where she was hiding.

"My goodness. But you're a shy one. Come over here Jane and I'll take a picture of the two of you together."

Surprisingly it was at that exact moment that the angel stood up, gracefully crossed the room and kissed me. It was only then that I realized I'd been admiring my own girlfriend!

Jane looked puzzled. "I pinned my hair back. Do you like it?"

I was speechless.

"You seem distracted Ray."

"You don't know the half of it." I muttered, thankful for Mrs. Rousseau's timing.

A decade later I moved to Calgary. One night at Marlborough Mall I heard a woman excitedly calling my name.

"Ray, Ray! I didn't know you'd moved out west. Wait until I tell Richard. He'll flip!

I didn't have a clue who she was. She chattered on endlessly about our mutual friends at university while I politely oohed and aahed about their latest adventures. Unfortunately, I couldn't remember a single one of them – not even her boyfriend Richard, who was supposedly one of my best friends. She gave me her number and I promised to put it 'somewhere safe.' When I got home I couldn't recollect where 'somewhere safe' was…Just as well, I still can't place her.

Things have only gotten worse recently. A few weeks ago, I popped into the newsroom where an attractive woman gave me a quick smile. I introduced myself. "Hi, I'm Ray. It's nice to meet you." She looked a bit perturbed.

"Don't you remember me?" she asked incredulously. "I used to type up all your articles and we talk at the front desk whenever you come in!"

I was mortified. I only wish Jane's mother had been there to save me. Luckily, the staff member in question is an extraordinarily nice human being. So I'm sure she'll forgive me – eventually. I don't want to embarrass her so I won't mention her name. Besides, I can't quite recall what it is.

As Rita Mae Brown said, "One of the keys to happiness is a bad memory."

If that's true, I should be downright ecstatic…

CHAPTER THREE:

STICKS AND STONES AND EDUCATION

"The trouble with learning from experience is that you never graduate."
~ Doug Larson ~

BACK TO SCHOOL

"Often, when reading a good book, I stop and thank my teacher. That is, I used to, until she got an unlisted number."

~ Author Unknown ~

When I was a child the worst day of the year was the Tuesday after Labour Day. The first day of school always engendered fear, loathing and despair. It was especially so when I was thirteen and entering high school.

When the alarm rang at six A.M. I was certain that there'd been a mistake. People aren't meant to get up at 6:00. Mom came in at 6:05 to make sure I was awake and like a young John McEnroe I muttered, "You can't be serious!"

Mom replied, "If you want to be a teacher someday, you'd better get used to it."

I stumbled to the kitchen already worried about essays and gym class and tests. The cat opened one eye and then smugly curled up and went back to sleep. I made a mental note. Someone was getting kibble not *Nine Lives* tonight.

After breakfast, quickly nearing an emotional precipice, I tried to pull myself together. "Maybe it won't be so bad. At least I'll make some new friends. Most people seem to like me," I ventured.

"Well you think they like you, which in your case is probably just as good," my brother quipped. That one broke Dad up. Even the dog was snickering as she ambled by to her dish.

"Hey Mom. I think the dog might have fleas," I retaliated.

"Oh dear, maybe we should give her a bath..." Her voice trailed off. At the word 'bath,' the dog beat a hasty retreat to the basement. I don't take sarcasm from anyone - especially someone with four legs. Besides, it's a jungle in the kitchen when you're thirteen.

My first class was introductory physics. The teacher gave us a twenty-minute lecture and then a pop quiz. I hadn't even had a coffee yet. Unfortunately, Mr. 'Einstein' had a penchant for trick questions. His tests were multiple choice but he always made us choose the alternative that was the 'most' correct. For example:

1) Light:
   a) Displays particle-like behaviour
   b) Displays wave-like behaviour
   c) Both*
   d) Neither in keeping with classical physics
   *The correct answer

Mr. 'Einstein' always subtracted the wrong answers from the right...or the right from the wrong in my case.

Looking back I think he may have scarred me for life. I still can't look at a slide rule without sobbing uncontrollably.

My second class was English. Mr. 'Picket' began by rolling up his pants and showing us his legs. "Eat your hearts out, girls!" he boasted. He'd been a teacher for twenty-five years. I quickly realized that the stress of teaching had done evil things to that old man. I resolved to choose a less demanding occupation: maybe a bomb disposal expert or an air traffic controller.

Luckily, not all of my instructors were that eccentric so I did manage to survive the first day of high school. I look back at it now with a hint of nostalgia. I was convinced that I'd have all of life's mysteries figured out by the time I graduated. But a lot of questions still remain:

<u>Five Questions Without Answers:</u>

1) If spelling is really so important why did they put a Parksville, B.C. school on the corner of 'Reid' and 'Wright' Roads?

2) If buffaloes can't fly, why are their wings served in the cafeteria?

3) Basic anatomy confirms that women have more fat than men. So the next time the Titanic goes down shouldn't we save a spot on the lifeboat for Leonardo DiCaprio and let Kate Winslet swim for it?

4) Do you really want a shop teacher with seven fingers?

5) If your Philosophy teacher tells you that he's a chronic liar, should you believe him?

In the end I never did get my teaching certificate. When people ask me why, I always reply, "I guess I didn't have the legs for it."
Thanks Mr. Picket.

The Rink

"Blessed are those who nought expect. For they shall not be disappointed."
~ Walcot ~

I never asked Dad to build us a tennis court.

When I was little I was the best hockey player on Sophia Drive. There wasn't a seven-year old who could touch me. There was just one problem: Mom and Dad wouldn't let me play in a league until I was nine. So I began a campaign to convince my Dad to build a rink in the backyard.

My Dad wasn't in any hurry to have a rink rat in the family. After all he was already working sixty hours a week and he wasn't enamored with the thought of endless early morning practices and weekend hockey tournaments. But after much cajoling and pleading he agreed to "think about it."

The next day at school I began bragging to my friends that Dad was going to build a full-scale replica of Maple Leaf Gardens in our yard. "Yes sir, boys, we're going to have red lines and blue lines and concession stands and a penalty box." There would be luxury seating for VIPs and standing room for less important people. That's where the stupid neighbourhood girls would have to stand - especially all the stupid teenage girls who used to hang around the house and make goo goo eyes at my brother. They wouldn't give me the time of day. Still don't...stupid girls.

My friend Ritchie doubted me. "Ray how can you fit Maple Leaf Gardens into your back yard? It's so small."

"My Dad will make it fit."

"How will he make the boards curve? He'd need an incredible tool. Yup, an incredible tool!"

"He's got a new hedge trimmer."

"My cousin says it took more than a year to build the Gardens with carpenters working around the clock."

"My Dad doesn't need to sleep."

"But it'll cost more than a million dollars!"

"He could get a second job. You'll see. He'll get the money!"

"A million dollars?"

"Yeah well, my brother can help. He wastes all his allowance on stupid girls."

That night I went home and told my Dad, "None of the guys believe you can build a rink."

"Oh?"

"They say you're too poor."

"That's ridiculous. I make a pretty good living."

"They say it would take you a year because you sleep too much."

"What?"

"And they say you're too stupid to put up the boards!"

"Who said that?"

"Ritchie. He says you're an 'incredible tool!'"

"We'll see about that! Saturday morning we'll build your rink. You tell your friends to be here Saturday afternoon and to bring their skates."

Early Saturday morning after breakfast Dad went down to the basement to get a hose, seven two by fours, a saw, some spikes and a roll of plastic. Strangely he didn't bring the hedge trimmer with him. Then we went outside and surveyed the yard. It was minus 15 outside and I wondered how he was going to keep the fans warm.

"Dad where are you going to put the furnace?"

Dad looked at me like I was from Mars. "Hold the end of the plastic."

A few minutes later he laid a section 4 feet by 24 feet on top of the patio. He positioned the 2x4's along the length - three per side - and cut the final 2x4 exactly in half. Reaching for the spikes, he 'toe nailed' all the pieces together. Finally, he turned on the tap, handed me the hose and said, "Start watering." The process took exactly 23 minutes.

I was out there for another hour before I realized Dad was done for the day. There would be no Maple Leaf Gardens, no curved boards and no concession stand.

That afternoon my friends began arriving to marvel at the edifice on Sophia Drive. My Dad came outside and proudly asked, " So what do you boys think of the rink?

I ran into the house. Later that evening Dad whispered to Mom, "He was so happy to have a rink he almost cried! I'll have to build him one every year."

And that's why I never asked Dad to build us a tennis court.

The Thunder Hunters

"Those who do not learn from history are doomed to repeat it."
~ George Santayana ~

A teacher once told me that "a journey of a thousand miles begins with a single step." He was very wise. But in the long run it isn't how many steps you take - it's what you step on that counts.

My father had little patience for foolish children. There is an old saying in Ecclesiastes that an ultimate fool is always "chasing after the wind." In Dutch they're called "donder jagers" or more literally, "thunder hunters." If my father called you a thunder hunter, you knew he'd reached the end of his patience.

As a young boy I had energy to burn. But as I ran around the backyard pretending to be Superman, I had the unfortunate habit of stepping in doggie doodoo. Not exactly superhero behaviour. Whether we played in the park, the backyard or the street; someway, somewhere, somehow, I always stepped in some of it – much to my father's annoyance. What followed would be a long process or removing the evidence from the bottom of my shoes with twigs and leaves and then finally soap and water. Dad always made me do it myself.

"You stepped in it. You clean it up. Thunder hunter!"

On weekends, Dad often took my brother and me fishing. Dad was a good fisherman using various different types of bait. Jay and I used worms - which he made us dig for ourselves in the backyard.

One afternoon Dad was in a hurry and decided to buy our worms at the dock.

"The marina is not a place for boys. Stay in the car."

A few moments later, Jay jumped out of the passenger seat and shouted, "You heard Dad. This is man's work. Stay in the car."

I fumed for a couple of minutes and then haughtily turned to the dog, "This is man's work, stay in the car." I started to run up the wooden sidewalk but Dad and Jay were already returning. I jumped into the backseat in just the nick of time. As we drove off, I began to notice a peculiar but familiar odour. I gave the dog an accusatory stare. She smiled back innocently. A few minutes later the smell reached the front seat.

Dad turned around.

"It wasn't me!"

Dad pulled over. "Everyone out of the car and check your shoes."

Dad's shoes were clean, Jay's were spotless and even the dog's paws were positively pristine. Dad stared at me. I held up my right runner. It looked like I'd stepped on a waffle.

"I told you to stay in the car!"

"But I stayed on the sidewalk," I mumbled.

"Thunder hunter," Dad said to no one in particular.

"Thunder hunter," Jay agreed sadly.

Dad and Jay enjoyed a fine afternoon dipping their lines in the water. I spent mine dipping my shoes in the lake.

When I was twelve, Jay began taking a keen interest in my thunder hunting too. It started one afternoon when I teased his girlfriend about her latest haircut. A little while later she and Jay were whispering together conspiratorially.

That night Jay remarked, "Hey Dad, how come Ray's hair is thinning?"

Dad muttered something under his breath and picked up the newspaper.

I ran to the mirror. "Bald? Me? But I'm only twelve."

"Yeah but Uncle Pete is bald. He went bald when he was twelve, didn't he Dad?"

Dad was engrossed in his paper and said nothing. I began feeling a rising sense of panic. Dad hadn't denied it. I spent the entire evening checking my hair in the mirror. Watching my performance Jay's girlfriend remarked, "Of all the children I've ever met, Ray is without doubt the most vain."

Jay nodded sadly, "Unbelievable, isn't it?"

For the next several weeks I wore my baseball cap everywhere I went. I'd been thoroughly had! Still, I guess it's never too early to learn that a man and his hair are soon parted. It's also helpful to remember there is more than one way to step in it.

I thought all of that was behind me until a few months ago when Jay and I went to look at a house together. As we walked into the backyard he turned to me and said, "We don't want any accidents. Remember to look for what the dog left behind."

Insulted, I replied, "I'm not seven anymore. Look for yourself."

A few seconds later, I was looking for twigs. I already now what Dad would have said, "Thunder Hunter!"

Jay dropped me off at home. He seemed enormously happy to get my sneakers out of his truck. As I walked up the driveway on my socks, he gave me a curious look.

"What?"

"Nothing. I just never noticed that bald spot before."

"Bald spot?" I asked, my voice quaking.

"I wouldn't worry about it. It's only about 4 inches in diameter."

"Four inches!" I exclaimed.

I quickly tried to look at the back of my head. I began turning in tighter and tighter circles until I looked like a poodle chasing its tail. By the way, no matter how fast you revolve, you can't see the back of your head! When I finally got to the bathroom and checked myself out with a hand mirror, I breathed a sigh of relief.

Then it dawned on me. Jay was pretty good at thunder hunting too.

I guess a journey of a thousand miles really does start with a single step. And what have I learned along the way? That George Santayana was right. "Those who don't learn from history are doomed to repeat it." No matter how often they step in it.

IMPRESSING MISS WRITE

"I had a terrible education. I attended a school for emotionally disturbed teachers."
~ Woody Allen ~

There are three types of liars in the world: fibbers, falsifiers and fabricators.

When I was eight I was in love with Miss Write. She was the sweetest third grade teacher a boy could have and I wanted nothing more than to impress her. But in a class of twenty-six students that wasn't an easy chore.

Just before Christmas, Miss Write gave us an assignment. "Now children," she said. "I want each of you to prepare a speech over the holidays. It should be at least 3 minutes long and it must have a theme. For example, you could talk about the life of Alexander Graham Bell. Naturally you would begin the speech with the year he was born and then discuss his early life and how he invented the telephone. Of course, the topic is up to you. We'll have all the speeches on the day we get back from Christmas vacation. Speeches will be given in alphabetical order. Julie Adams will be first and Jimmy Worthington will be last." Then she dismissed the class and sent us home.

Over Christmas I spent a lot of time thinking about my speech. I daydreamed about Miss Write's thunder struck reaction when I delivered the best speech she'd ever heard about Alexander Graham Bell. "Oh Ray!" she'd coo. "Someday you'll be president."

"No, Miss Write, I'll be prime minister. Canada doesn't have a president. We learned that last week in history class."

"Oh Ray, You know everything! And you're so strong too!"

"Yes I am, Miss Write. Yes I am."

Christmas holidays ended with the resumption of school on January 3rd. On January 2nd I started to write my speech. I got the old encyclopedia out of the basement and turned to the section on Alexander Graham Bell. It began:

"Alexander Graham Bell was born on March 3, 1847 in Edinburgh, Scotland. Mr. Bell is best known for his invention of the telephone. He also worked on several other inventions including the wheat husk remover…" I turned to the next page and to my dismay it read, "Andrew Bell was an educator born in 1753. He invented an educational system called the monitorial system."

A whole page was missing from the encyclopedia! What could I do? It was Sunday and the town library was closed. Not allowing myself to become flustered, I decided to do some research around the house. I wandered into the kitchen. Let's see. The article said something about wheat husks. I looked in the cupboard and found some surprisingly relevant information. Then I looked into Dad's liquor cabinet and found some more. Finally I went to the phone and in no time my speech was written. I practiced it all that afternoon in my room:

"Alexander Graham Bell was born on March 3, 1847 in Edinburgh, Scotland. Mr. Bell is best known for his invention of the telephone. He also worked on several other inventions including the wheat husk remover. Many people aren't aware that Mr. Bell was the inventor of the *Graham Cracker,*' which is made out of wheat. You may also be unaware that Mr. Bell was the inventor of the *Brandy Alexander.*'

My Dad says that many adults are grateful for the invention of the *Brandy Alexander.*' He also says that the man who invented the Brandy Alexander was a saint. So I guess that's why the Pope named him Saint Alexander. They must drink a lot of those in Russia because they named a whole town Saint Alexander over there. But I'm not sure if they have phones.

Although Mr. Bell was born in Scotland, few people know he was Japanese. That information is printed on his phone, which clearly says, *'Made in Japan.'*

Let us now discuss his invention of the church bell, the Bell organ and my personal favourite: the taco, which is available at his excellent chain of restaurants known as Taco Bell..."

It went on from there. The next morning I was off to school. I was 25th in alphabetical order in my class. I stopped along the way and talked to Jimmy Worthington.

"What's your speech about, Jimmy?"

"Alexander Graham Bell."

"Me too. But you're so lucky. You get to go last!"

Class started promptly at nine. After opening exercises Miss Write smiled and said, "It's time for your speeches. We'll begin with Julie Adams."

Julie went up to the front of the class and with great self-assurance began her presentation:

"Alexander Graham Bell was born on March 3, 1847 in Edinburgh, Scotland. Mr. Bell is best known for his invention of the telephone."

After she finished we all applauded and Miss Write gave her an A. The next speech was from Jeremy Anderson. He began:

"Alexander Graham Bell was born on March 3, 1847 in Edinburgh, Scotland. Mr. Bell is best known for his invention of the telephone."

Miss Write seemed perplexed but we continued on. A total of twenty-four children gave their speeches. And all twenty-four speeches were about Alexander Graham Bell. Still, I was confident because no one else had mentioned his Taco Bell franchise or the Graham cracker. Miss Write called me to the front of the class.

"Alexander Graham Bell was born on March 3, 1847 in Edinburgh, Scotland. Mr. Bell is best known for his invention of the telephone. He also worked on several other inventions including the wheat husk…"

Just then there was a horrendous noise. It was Miss Write slamming her ruler on the desk. "No!" she said. "No more. Sit down. You get an F. I don't want to hear one more word about Alexander Graham Bell!"

I was crestfallen but grateful not to be Jimmy Worthington. Miss Write towered over his desk and putting her face close to his demanded, "What is your speech about, Jimmy?"

Jimmy looked at her helplessly.

"What is your speech about?"

Jimmy looked like an antelope separated from the herd by a particularly hungry cheetah. I noticed a puddle was beginning to form under his desk.

"What is your speech about?"

"Bedwetting," he replied and then asked to be excused.

Miss Write was never the same after that morning. She eventually gave up teaching and had a successful second career as a vindictive childless spinster. Jimmy is a successful urologist. As for me, my mission in life is to reveal the shocking truth behind the legend of Alexander Graham Bell. Which brings me back to my original point: There are three types of liars in the world: fibbers, falsifiers and fabricators. And the worst of these are humour columnists.

EVERYONE IS MY COUNSELLOR

"Every man I meet is my superior in some way. In that I learn of (from) him."
~ Ralph Waldo Emerson ~

When I was in 18, I wanted to change the world. I believed deeply in love, compassion and Christian values. However, like most 18 year-olds, I had a lot to learn about the real world and my place in it.

My friend Brad and I were looking for summer jobs when we discovered that several positions were available at a project for the developmentally disabled. Although neither one of us had any experience in that area we immediately signed up for interviews.

When we arrived at the group home we were escorted to a large recreation room and told to wait. A few minutes later twenty-two developmentally disabled adults came streaming in. I had seldom been exposed to people with disabilities before and it was scary. But, in retrospect, I doubt anyone could devise a better interview. Sink or swim, it was that simple. Brad and I got involved in the activities and soon found that we were enjoying ourselves. Luckily, we were both hired.

That was the summer I fell in love with Jane, who was one of the other counsellors. Jane had an eight-year-old brother with Down's syndrome. Ted was the absolute center of Jane's household with a mischievous laugh and an impish grin that could melt anyone's heart. Ted's language skills were limited and sometimes in his overwhelming desire to speak like an adult he would pretend to use big words. Unfortunately, the sounds he made were unintelligible. To help him develop normal speaking skills we were asked to say, "Ted, don't talk baby talk," every time he used pretend words. We didn't realize how often Ted heard this phrase until late one afternoon while he was playing next to the phone. Jane's father, a physician, was calling in a series of prescriptions to the local pharmacist. As he read off the names of the various drugs, Ted looked up at him sternly and said, "Dad, don't talk baby talk!"

That summer flew by. I don't know who had more fun, the trainees or the twelve teenaged counsellors who were there to instruct them. We played baseball, took them swimming and did endless crafts (I can still hook a pretty mean rug). Yes, it was one long happy summer. And as it progressed, we counsellors began to feel pretty self-satisfied. I began to think of myself as a *counsellor* with a capital C: a force for good imparting spiritual wisdom to the less fortunate. That is until one morning in August.

When we arrived for work, we were told that one of the trainees, Duncan, was being punished and would not be allowed to eat lunch. The group home was solemn and we were all pretty upset about the use of food as a punishment. (Luckily this type of correction is no longer allowed). We resolved to continue on with our normal activities but our hearts weren't in them.

I was sitting in the park when Duncan came and sat next to me. Duncan had always been my favorite trainee. He looked very much like Jerry Lewis in *The Nutty Professor* and wore thick horn-rimmed glasses that perched precariously on the tip of his nose. He had a severe intellectual impairment and I was worried about how he was handling his punishment. What wisdom could I impart? As I pondered how to help him, I felt a hand on my shoulder. It was Duncan's. He leaned in close to me and said, "We believe in God, Ray. Everything will be all right."

I heard a quote once on an old *All In The Family* episode. "Every man I meet is my superior that I might learn from him." I later found out it was a paraphrase of Ralph Waldo Emerson. After that morning I stopped thinking of myself as a champion of the disabled. I began instead to view developmentally challenged people as just that: people. Duncan taught me more about courage and faith that morning that any textbook or university professor ever could.

Since then, I've met a lot of people with developmental disabilities. There was Cedric who was probably the best cribbage player I ever played and took particular delight in skunking me. He taught me to take joy in the game, even when you don't win.

There was Peter who always knew when someone was sad and invariably found some way to cheer them up. Peter had a vocabulary of just a few words. But his compassionate heart spoke loud and clear. He taught me that the best counselling tools are empathy and love.

There was Jake who had been institutionalized for fifty difficult years. He moved into my family's group home when he was nearly seventy. He had a winning smile and enjoyed dancing. He never raised his voice in anger. But when someone asked him what he thought of the institution he whispered, "They oughta burn it to the ground!" It was the only time I ever heard him complain. He taught me the wisdom of putting the past behind you.

After that golden summer my career path was clear. I've spent most of my adult life working with developmentally challenged people either as a staff member or volunteer. I often received the lofty title of '*counsellor*' while they were referred to as '*trainees*' or '*clients*.' But they were helping me just as much as I was helping them. And each one had a special gift to share.

To paraphrase Emerson, " Everyone I meet is my *counsellor*. Because I may learn from them."

Indeed.

CHAPTER FOUR:

IN THE SPIRIT

*"No man ever believes that the Bible means what it says.
He is always convinced that it says what he means."*
~ George Bernard Shaw ~

Careless Words

*"I tell you that on the Day of Judgment
people will render account for every careless word they
utter."*
~ Matthew 12:36 ~

When I was a child I learned a simple rhyme in school:
'Sticks and stones may break my bones but names will
never hurt me.' I never questioned it. In fact, it gave me
license to make fun of my friends and for them to
reciprocate. In our little world any joke was fair game –
no matter how cruel - as long as it was funny.

My Dad didn't care for my put-downs. One afternoon
he explained why. Some months earlier he had taken
Mom to the supermarket. While Mom examined the
produce, Dad began making fun of the other shoppers.
Mom shushed him but Dad ignored her. After all, he was
speaking Dutch so who'd know? As they turned the
corner there was an especially fat woman in front of them.

Dad snorted, "Bekijk die grote vette vrouw voor ons. Ik wedde zij haar eigen postcode heeft." Roughly translated it means, "Look at that great big fat woman in front of us. I bet she has her own postal code."

Mom gave him a disapproving look. But Dad chortled safe in the knowledge that his bon mot was hidden behind an impenetrable language barrier. Suddenly the woman whirled her cart around. Looking Dad square in the eye she responded in fluent Dutch, "Ik ben vet maar u bent ruw." Which means, "I'm fat but you're very rude." Mortified, Dad beat a hasty retreat to the car. Careless words.

Dad told that story again and again at parties and family gatherings. I suppose it was a kind of penance for hurting that lady's feelings. But the moral was lost on me. At least until I was fourteen:

When I was in junior high school the currency of our popularity was meted out in put-downs and insults. One afternoon Sidney and I took aim at each other in gym class. I was determined to prevail but he held the upper hand ripping me with one-liners. Later, the teacher divided us into two teams for basketball: shirts and skins. Unfortunately for Sid, he was one of the skins.

One of nature's tricks on some adolescent boys is the temporary development of fatty deposits on their chests. At fourteen Sidney was, to put it mildly, well endowed. Instinctively I moved in for the kill. "Hey Sidney, how does it feel to buy your clothes in the Young Miss department? Is your girlfriend jealous?"

The gymnasium erupted with laughter. Victory was mine! Basking in its glow I glanced over at Sid expecting an acknowledgement of my sarcastic prowess. Instead he was staring at the floor. As he bit his lip I realized he was trying very hard not to cry. Careless words.

In my third year of university, Dad suffered a massive heart attack. Despite bypass surgery it was soon obvious he was failing. One afternoon the class was discussing 19th century English novels. The professor began asking questions but I was miles away. Suddenly we were face to face.

"In Dickens' work who does this female character represent?"

I had no idea to which female character he was referring but took a wild guess. "She could be an earth mother."

There was a tittering in the auditorium.

"Madame Lafarge?" he asked incredulously.

"She could be," I repeated helplessly.

"An earth mother?"

"Could be," I whispered, my voice trailing off.

Steve, a student known for his acidic wit retorted, "She 'could' be the bloody quarterback for the Green Bay Packers! But that wouldn't make you any less of an idiot." The entire auditorium broke out in riotous laughter. Even the professor was snickering. A few days later my father passed away. Careless words.

Sometimes our most regrettable words seem the most innocent. In a small town near Medicine Hat, Alberta there was an old-fashioned general store. A man I'll call Mr. Wildman owned it. Known as Mr. Herman to his friends, he was a genuinely nice septuagenarian, well read and gregarious. Sometimes folks would come in and ask Mr. Wildman if they could put their grocery order on credit. Mr. Wildman would always smile and say, "Sure, we'll settle up at the end of the month." One afternoon my brother and I watched surreptiously as a poor family signed their credit slip. Mr. Wildman waited until they were safely outside then quietly threw their slip in the garbage. I wonder how many children would have gone hungry in that little town if not for Mr. Herman?

One night I popped into the store at closing time. My brother Jay was buying a bottle of pop. We were the only customers there. Instead of locking up, Mr. Herman invited us to sit down and chat. He was in a reflective mood and I could sense he didn't want to be alone.

"Did I ever tell you about my experiences during the war?"

I was tired and hungry and wanted to get home. "How 'bout you tell me tomorrow, Mr. Herman?"

He seemed disappointed but offered me a cordial goodnight. Jay stayed a while listening to his stories. The next morning I dashed up to the store for some cereal. The doors were locked and a several seniors were commiserating outside. Mr. Herman had died in his sleep. "How 'bout you tell me tomorrow, Mr. Herman?" Careless words.

I'll remember Mr. Herman, Sid and Steve for the rest of my days. They remind me of the shortness of life, the shallowness of conquest and the singular fragility of the human heart.

"I tell you that on the Day of Judgment people will render account for every careless word they utter."

Sometimes sooner.

I Do Solemnly Wear

'Angels can fly because they take themselves lightly.'
-G.K. Chesterton-

When I was little, our family wasn't known for its church-going habits. Although respectful, my brother and I were not always prepared for the solemnity of religion.

When Jay was five, he was invited to supper at a Catholic neighbour's house. When he returned home, he had a pensive look and my mother asked him what was the matter.

"Well," he said. "Before we ate everyone put their heads down and closed their eyes real tight!"

"Do you know why they did that?"

"At first, I thought we were all going to smell the food and guess what we were eating."

"But that's not what they did?"

"No."

"So what do you think they were doing?"

"I suppose they were all thinking about how good a cook Mrs. Thibault is and how grateful we should be for supper."

Not a bad definition of grace from a five year-old.

I never worried about my own light-hearted view of religion until I was thirteen. One day our Grade Nine history teacher gave us a pop quiz on Hebrew civilization. I'm sure many a theologian would be surprised to discover that the Bible was divided into the First and Second Testaments; the Jewish people lived in Menorahs and

Samson, by virtue of his long hair, was the first hippie. Obviously, I needed a more solemn and informed approach to faith.

When I was 17, I had a life changing, born again experience. Soon after, I joined a local church. One afternoon, the minister asked my friend Jerry and I to prepare a skit based on the Prodigal Son. I played the father and Jerry was the prodigal. When Sunday morning came, the minister read from Luke Chapter 15 as Jerry entered the Church:

"*But while he was still a long way off, his father saw him and was filled with compassion for him; he ran to his son, threw his arms around him and kissed him.*"

When I saw Jerry, I jumped off the stage and ran down the aisle with all the velocity of a linebacker. Unable to brake in time, I hit him at nearly full speed and knocked him for a two-yard loss. Strangely, it was the last play they asked me to perform in.

When I reached adulthood, I was determined to become more solemn and to tone down my ebullient nature. While working on a local United Way Campaign I met a Mennonite minister and we soon became friends. One Sunday, he invited me to come to church. I arrived with just the right note of propriety wearing dress pants, a jacket and a tie. The pants were too small for me but they were the only pair I had that went with the jacket. No matter, they created the proper conservative image.

I began to introduce myself to the other parishioners and was pleasantly surprised by their reactions. I was staid and serious, not at all my usual enthusiastic joke-cracking self, and yet they were still smiling! Yes, practically everyone I met grinned broadly when I approached. Many young women giggled and a few turned red. Being single, I guessed my minister friend had put in a good word for me with the ladies of the church. Still, I was slightly confused why so many people were asking me if I was cold on such a beautiful spring day.

After the service, I headed down to the coffee room where I happened to pass a mirror. Wearing decidedly too small dress pants had produced an unexpected side effect. My fly was down. It was humiliating. But looking back, I think God was teaching me not to take myself too seriously. It's a lesson I haven't forgotten.

"Angels can fly because they take themselves lightly."
Words to live by.

Past Imperfect

"Prediction is very difficult, especially if it's about the future."
~Nils Bohr~

We all have them - high hopes for the future; dreams of fame, money and romance. And most of us have well-meaning friends who predict our certain failure if we try to achieve them. In essence, they are prophesying the future. Since prophecy is an ancient art, let's take a look at some famous prophets throughout the ages:

There are literally thousands of Old Testament prophecies that have been fulfilled. But Bible prophets lived by a different set of rules than modern day prophets. If they messed up even once, they were stoned to death. A pretty tough standard but it did keep out the riff-raff.

Take Baalam, for instance. He was a Canaanite false prophet. He cursed people for a living. These days he'd probably be a shock jock. One morning his donkey stopped suddenly and refused to continue. Balaam was ticked. What he didn't know was that there was an angel up ahead preparing to kill him. The donkey knew. Baalam, no member of PETA, started beating on the poor defenseless creature. Not happy with Balaam's behaviour, God granted the donkey the gift of speech. It promptly turned around and gave Baalam heck for being such a creep. And that dear reader was the first time in recorded history an ass ever offered his opinion. Unfortunately it wasn't the last...

Prophets weren't just around in biblical times. The nineteenth century was full of them. Lord Kelvin was a renowned physicist and mathematician. But he's most famous for his prophecy that heavier-than-air flying machines would be 'impossible' given the laws of physics. I guess poor Orville and Wilbur Wright never studied law. They were too busy inventing the airplane.

Then there was Dr. Pierre Pachet, famous British surgeon and Professor of Physiology. Pachet's contribution to the world of prophecy was the following: "Louis Pasteur's theory of germs is ridiculous fiction."

Now, I'm no scientist but I think a doctor should wash his hands before he asks me to say, "Ah!" Mind you, I may be obsessing.

Still, it isn't just the fields of science and religion that expose the folly of false prophets. Recent history is replete with examples. Take for instance, Jim Denny, manager of the Grand Ole Opry. He reportedly told a young Elvis Presley to go back to driving a truck. I wonder what ever happened to that kid from Tupelo?

Dick Rowe, former head of Decca Records is another example. Given the chance to sign the Beatles in 1962, Dick declined, blithely prophesying that guitar groups were 'on their way out.' A few months later, Beatle George Harrison told Rowe about another up and coming British band. Rowe took George's advice and signed them immediately. You may have heard of them. They're called *The Rolling Stones*. I wonder if he ever sent George a thank you card?

Modern day prophets call themselves 'psychics.' Every year in supermarket tabloids they make stunning predictions. Unlike Bible prophets, their predictions never come true. So far as I know, colonies of space aliens have not stolen all our oil - although that might explain the price of unleaded. Nor has the West Coast fallen into the Pacific. So, if you bought 'ocean front' property in Calgary or Phoenix, you're out of luck. And, of course, no living dinosaur has been seen this year – unless you count Mick Jagger.

After reading those whoppers I'm pretty sure the only reason psychics aren't being stoned these days is because most of them are 'stoned' already.

I don't worry about people's predictions. When they tell me I'll never be voted the sexiest man alive, I just laugh. I cry too - but that's a story for my therapist.

When they say I'll never be a recording artist, I pull out my guitar and cassette deck and practice the *Pollywog Song*. Justin Bieber eat your heart out.

And when they predict that I'll never win the Nobel Prize for literature, I just remember that Martin Luther said, "There is no limit to this fever for writing; every one must be an author; some out of vanity, to acquire celebrity and raise up a name, others for the sake of mere gain."

And he was so right!

So if Danielle Steele, John Grisham and Stephen King would just retire already, there'd be plenty of room for me at the top of the New York Times Bestseller List.

That's what I'm predicting anyway.

MIDNIGHT IN PARADISE

"All dogs go to heaven."
~ Caroline Thompson ~

A lay preacher once told me that dogs couldn't go to heaven because they don't have souls. I wonder:

When I was ten, I desperately wanted a dog. I cajoled, I begged and I pleaded. Finally my parents relented.

"If we get you a dog you'll have to feed it, walk it and clean up the poop," my Dad sternly warned. I quickly agreed.

"I'll be just like 'Timmy' on the 'Lassie Show.' She'll sleep in my room; we'll solve crimes and rescue Mom from coyotes.

Dad gave me a withering look. "There are no coyotes in Toronto."

"Yeah but if there were, my dog and I would save her." I could hardly wait for 'Lassie' to come home.

A few weeks later my folks bought a beautiful one year-old Labrador retriever. Frightened by her new surroundings, she nervously paced back and forth emitting remarkably odious flatulence. Not exactly Lassie type behaviour.

Dad opened a window and asked, "What shall we name her?"

"How about Windy?" my brother chortled.

"No," Mom said kindly. "She's been through enough changes. We'll just keep the name she already has: Midnight."

Over the next few weeks Mom made a special effort to make Midnight feel at home: brushing her, taking her for walks and giving her special treats. Before long she was one of the family. But it was clear that it was my mother who had won her heart.

Since Midnight was officially my dog, I thought she should sleep in my room. But every night at nine o'clock she would quietly slip away. Where she slept was a mystery. One afternoon Dad noticed a pile of black hair on the old couch downstairs. That night he pretended to watch television but kept an eye open. At nine o'clock, Midnight quietly inched toward the stairs pausing at the top to make sure no one was watching. Dad waited for about twenty minutes and motioned for us to follow him to the basement. He flicked on the lights and there was Midnight luxuriously stretched out on the couch like a self-indulgent movie star. The jig was up. But before Dad could dispense any punishment, Mom started to laugh. Then Dad started laughing too. Mom gave Midnight a hug and whispered, "It's all right sweetie, you can sleep here."

I've never seen a more grateful – or confused - dog in my life.

About a week later Mom and Dad threw a party. A young woman wearing a short mini skirt was sitting on the newly vacuumed couch in the basement. About nine o'clock Midnight came downstairs. She surveyed the room, trotted over and began to repeatedly push her cold nose against the young lady's bare leg.

"What on earth is wrong with your dog?" she exclaimed.

I replied, "It's Midnight's bedtime. That's her mattress you're sitting on."

"Ewwwww!" she exclaimed.

"She's as clean as I am," I protested. My Dad gave me a menacing look and I retreated upstairs. Adults were so confusing.

Every weekend, Dad would drive us up to Lake Simcoe. As soon as we arrived Midnight would make a beeline for the water. By the time we got the car unloaded she'd be back at the cottage, soaking wet from her chest down. The next Saturday, curious about her behaviour, Dad put Midnight on a leash and led her to the water. When he let her off the lead, she jumped right into the lake and then sat down. Several seconds later something floated up behind her that I normally picked up with a shovel.

"Wow. Gross!" exclaimed my brother.

"Crazy dog!" said Dad, shaking his head in disbelief.

"She's no 'Lassie,'" I muttered.

Mom said nothing for a few minutes. Then she suggested that my brother and I wait a while before swimming. Moms always know what to say.

Midnight's favourite activity was playing catch. I'd throw her old tennis ball and she'd bring it back. After all, she was a retriever. One afternoon, Dad punished me for some infraction and I was feeling sorry for myself. In a moment of frustration, I threw the ball a lot harder than I meant too and it whizzed just past her eye. Another half inch and I could have seriously hurt her. Now if someone had thrown that ball at me I would have been incensed. But Midnight just looked bewildered. Then she ran over to me pushing her nose into my hand as if to ask me what was wrong. I've never forgotten my careless temper tantrum or that 'dumb' animal's act of forgiveness. I was no 'Timmy.'

When Midnight was twelve, my father died. By then her muzzle was gray and she was plagued by heart and kidney disease. But she still looked out for my mother, following her from room to room and growling whenever strangers came to the door.

Eighteen months later, Mom began to correspond with a gentleman from her old hometown. They wrote each other several times and agreed to meet. Mom said, "The moment he got out of his car, I knew he was the one." I guess Midnight knew it too. Because that very morning she died. Midnight had lived two years longer than the vet thought possible and she looked after Mom until the exact moment Henry arrived to take over the responsibility.

Do dogs have souls? I don't know but Midnight taught me more about loyalty, devotion and forgiveness than any person I've met. As for my friend the lay preacher, he clearly forgot about Isaiah 11:6-8 which unequivocally states that there will be animals in the afterlife. Lions and lambs anyway.

Do all dogs go to heaven? Only God knows for sure. But I sure hope there'll be a Midnight in Paradise.

God Will Not Be Silent

" I will not leave you as orphans..."
John 14:18:

There is a singular character trait I have observed in great men and great women of faith. It is the ability to be 'serious' while never taking themselves 'seriously.' And so it was with John Paul II.

He was a man renowned for his determined adherence to biblical principals and yet beloved for his self-effacing humour. He spoke out without compromise on 'conservative' moral issues but was equally fearless in his 'liberal' attacks on consumerism, unbridled capitalism and unjust war. Grace in the face of great suffering became his trademark.

Karol Józef Wojtyła was born in Wadowice, Poland in 1920. As a child he was both athletic and pious, so much so that the children in his class teased him with the moniker, 'apprentice saint.' He learned about suffering early in life losing his mother in 1929 and his only sibling, an older brother, in 1932. When his father died in 1941, he was inconsolable, crying next to the bedside for an entire day. Now seemingly alone in the world and facing a brutal German regime, he surreptitiously began studying for the priesthood. Forced into hard labour at a local quarry, he still pioneered a covert theatre troupe that promoted freedom during the Nazi occupation. He was ordained in 1946 and became archbishop of Crackow in

1958. Twenty years later to everyone's surprise he became Pope John Paul II.

Like so many renowned religious leaders, the pope knew how to have fun. Once when some Canadian schoolchildren visited the Vatican, he entertained them by doing a Charlie Chaplin impression complete with twirling cane. Another time, asked if a Pope could resign, he replied that he would likely consider it if only he knew where to send the letter of resignation.

It seems that a sense of humour is a common trait among people of great faith:

Billy Graham once told a story about leading a crusade in a small town. Before the services, he asked a young boy for directions to the federal building so he could mail a letter. Thanking the youngster, Billy told him that in return he should come to the Baptist church where Billy would give him directions to heaven. The boy replied incredulously, "I don't think I'll be there. You don't even know the way to the post office!"

Mother Teresa was indeed a serious woman, but she also had a great sense of the absurd. As she lay dying, her lawyer asked her what she wanted done about a man trying to sell a cinnamon bun (the Nunbun) which looked remarkably like her. She replied, "Tell him he will have to bake another that looks like my successor."

Pope John XXIII was famous for his sharp wit and humility. "It often happens that I wake at night and begin to think about a serious problem and decide I must tell the pope about it. Then I wake up completely and remember that I am the pope!"

And the famous and greatly honoured American preacher, Billy Sunday, once said, "Your reputation is what people say about you. Your character is what God and your wife know about you."

God will not be silent. In each generation he provides the religious leaders required to guide the faithful through perilous times. After the passing of Moses there was Joshua, after Elijah there was Elisha. Even after the resurrection of Christ, Peter and Paul were ordained to spread the gospel. In our time many remarkable people of faith have taken up the mantle of leadership: Pope John XXIII, Billy Graham and Mother Teresa to name a few. Each has inspired and changed the world for the better but none more so than Pope John Paul II.

The passing of John Paul II was a poignant one. But his legacy lives on. And so must we. "I will not leave you as orphans." God will not be silent.

CHAPTER FIVE:

OUR FAMILY TREE

"Some family trees bear an enormous crop of nuts."
~ Wayne H ~

THE TROUBLE WITH TAPIOCA

"Gratitude is the heart's memory."
~ French Proverb ~

My father knew how to tell a story. Every Sunday night over tapioca pudding he'd regale us with tales of his childhood and his exploits during the war. Dad never told us a story without a lesson or moral in it and some bear repeating:

I remember one evening Dad told us a story about gratitude. He began in a solemn voice, "When I was a young boy in Holland we were very poor. So poor that we often had to do without. I hated black beans but one night for dinner that's all there was. Your Grandma explained that we should be grateful for whatever food we get. But I was stubborn and wouldn't eat them. 'Fine,' she said, ' then you can go to bed without supper.'"

"I'll tell you boys I was so hungry the next morning that I could hardly wait for breakfast. Grandma ladled out porridge to my brothers and sisters but guess what was on my plate? Those same black beans! Well, I was as stubborn as Grandma and I refused to eat them. So off I went to school and by lunchtime, oh boy was I hungry. I opened up my lunch box. And guess what was inside… black beans! I was so hungry by then that I gave in and ate one. And you want to know something? It was pretty good so I ate them all. And when I got home Grandma asked, 'Enjoy your lunch, son?' And I said, 'Yes, Mama.' Now what have you boys learned from this story?"

My brother Jay exclaimed, "We don't ever want to go to Holland because Grandma will let us starve."

"No, no, no …you're missing the point. What about you, Ray?"

"Why didn't anybody at school share his lunch with you, Dad? Didn't you have any friends?"

"I had lots of friends. That's not the point."

"Boy, if all I had were some beans my friends would give me a sandwich. How come the other kids didn't like you?"

"They liked me fine. That's not the point…it's about gratitude. Oh never mind. Go out and play."

Another time my Dad sat us down to discuss pride. With great solemnity he began, "Listen up boys. I have an important lesson to teach you. When I was about eight my father was out of work and we didn't have any money. Well it so happened that my shoes began to wear out. Eventually they had to be thrown away even though we couldn't afford new ones. So I had to wear my mother's shoes to school. And let me tell you that was embarrassing! But I was grateful that my feet were dry.

And I held my head up high! I think you boys can learn something from this story. Do you have any questions?"

Jay said, "I saw a man on TV yesterday wearing women's shoes. They were high heels and he was singing like Judy Garland. Dad, can you sing like Judy Garland?"

"No, of course not!"

"The man on TV wore a dress? Did Grandma make you wear a dress too, Dad?

"No! You kids are missing the point again!"

"The man on TV shaved his legs. Do you shave your legs, Dad?

"No, absolutely not! Look I'm just trying to explain to you kids that you should be proud no matter what your station is in life."

"I don't remember what station he was on. Does that matter?"

"No. Look I just want you to follow my example."

"Does that mean we have to wear Mom's shoes?"

"Never mind. Just go play!"

One Sunday evening Dad taught us how to stand up to bullies. "Boys, it isn't easy being a sergeant in the army. You have a platoon of men and you have to turn them into soldiers. Now in my first command, I had a couple of goldbricks named Hans and Eric. Hans and Eric were always mouthing off. I couldn't put up with that or I would have lost the respect of the outfit. So I made them take four mile hikes with a full pack until they smartened up."

"What was the worse thing they did, Dad?"

"Well boys, they weren't only lazy but thieves too. On Sundays we'd get tapioca pudding and sometimes, I'd put my pudding in my locker for a late night snack…and if I turned my back for a minute my pudding would be gone.

"Why didn't you just lock your locker?"

"We didn't have locks on them in the army."

"Then why did they call them lockers?"

"I think we're drifting here. The point is they were stealing my pudding."

"So what did you do, Dad?"

"This will probably surprise you. But a man has to do what a man has to do. Boys, I'd spit in my pudding right in front of the whole platoon. And then I would go out for the evening and you know something…my pudding was always there when I came back! And when I took my pudding out and ate it everyone would laugh. You know why? Because they knew I'd bested Hans and Eric. I hope you boys have learned something from this story. Any questions?

Jay piped up, "Dad, how do you know that when you were gone Hans and Eric didn't spit in your pudding too?"

"Yeah," I added, "maybe all the guys who didn't like you took turns. Maybe that's why everybody was laughing."

Dad was quiet. A few seconds later his face began to turn an odd colour…it was a rather interesting shade of green. He motioned for us to go outside. Oddly that was the last time we had tapioca pudding with Sunday supper.

As I said, my Dad knew how to tell a story. Unlike my stories, his were scrupulously true. I've learned a lot from them. That's why to this day you'll never see me eating black beans and tapioca pudding in high heels while wearing a dress singing 'Over The Rainbow.' Thanks, Dad.

Kitty's Story

"The smallest feline is a masterpiece."
~ Leonardo Da Vinci ~

My brother Jay never wanted a cat. During the time we shared a house in the 1980's he was abundantly clear on that point. Nor is he the type of person who can be easily swayed on any subject once he makes up his mind. And that makes Kitty's story all the more remarkable.

Kitty was born on St. Patrick's Day 1983 but she didn't start out with the luck of the Irish. She was the runt of the litter. She had a troubling heart problem and was pretty much abandoned by the time she was six weeks old. But that's when her luck began to change.

Our friend Faith was providing a loving home for four cats when she heard about Kitty. And though there was no way she could take in another stray, she was bound and determined to save her. Faith knew all about Jay's cat edict but cheerfully insisted that Jay and Kitty were meant for each other. And even though I thought it was a waste of time, I agreed to bring Jay by for coffee.

When Jay and I arrived for our visit, Faith went to work. After coffee and small talk she opened the patio door and let Kitty in. She was an exceedingly beautiful kitten with tortoise shell markings. Tiny, with bright expressive eyes, she commanded our attention the way a model dominates a runway in Paris.

"Faith. Did you get another cat?" Jay asked.

"No," she replied. " She's not ours."

"Oh. Pretty little thing. Whose is she?"

"No one's," Faith replied adding just the right note of solemnity. "Poor kitten. She's probably going to be put down." And then Kitty, as if on cue, jumped into Jay's lap, slipped inside his jacket and began to purr contentedly.

"Put down? Why would anyone put her down?" Jay demanded.

"Because no one wants to adopt her," Faith replied.

Jay looked at the helpless little creature inside his jacket and with great gravitas declared, " I won't have it! I won't let someone destroy this kitten. I'll take her!"

"Well if you're sure," Faith replied with eyes twinkling.

Although Kitty took to life at Jay's house with great enthusiasm, she did need to unlearn a few of life's early lessons. Having lived most of her former life outside, she knew nothing about the comforts of home. During her first night with us we found her curled around the base of a potted fern in the living room. She had dug herself into the dirt: a trick she had obviously picked up to keep warm during her weeks of homelessness. It took days to convince her it was okay to sleep on the bed or the couch.

She also refused to drink water from her dish. We were both concerned she might become dehydrated until we discovered why. In the basement she'd found an old bucket. It was filled with stagnant water and that, of course, was what she was used to drinking. It again took days to convince her it was okay to drink fresh water from a clean dish.

After I moved into my apartment, Kitty took on new responsibilities in Jay's life. One morning she woke him up by bouncing up and down on his head. "Crazy cat," he muttered. What on earth?"

She made quite a fuss until he followed her out to the back window where the oilman was filling the tank. Well, no cat in the history of the world received more praise than Kitty did that morning. She also received some canned tuna – one of her favourite treats. Jay phoned me later to brag about his "watch cat." The next day Kitty woke Jay up by bouncing on his head again. He stumbled to the back window and saw the meter reader. Again Kitty received great praise and more tuna. The day after Kitty repeated the process. When Jay looked out the back window there was a cat in the yard. The following day it was a bird. The next day there was a squirrel. Although Kitty took her responsibilities seriously, she apparently didn't differentiate between species. I got no further calls from my brother bragging about his "watch cat" and I'm pretty sure Kitty didn't get any more early morning tuna either.

A few years later my brother bought a house in the country. I was visiting one day when a mouse ran through the open front door into his kitchen and underneath the stove. We were discussing how to remove the mouse when Kitty joined us in the kitchen to see what all the fuss was about. The mouse, deciding that the underside of a stove was no longer a safe place to hide, made a break for it unintentionally ending up face to face with the cat. Kitty took one look at the mouse, jumped back at least three feet, turned tail and ran. Jay watched her with disgust and muttered, "My hero."

For many years my brother worked a night shift. He would sleep during the day and leave for work in the late afternoon. I came for a visit one week and discovered Kitty's part in his routine. At 3 PM she began getting agitated. Then she ran up and down the hall in front of his bedroom and then pushed open his door. Then she ran into the bedroom at a speed I'd never seen her attain before. Achieving maximum velocity she careened into the side of the bed the way a racecar slams into a corner at the Indy 500 and then exploded out of the room again. After about a two-minute wait the process was repeated until Jay got up and stumbled into the shower to start his day. When I asked him about it later, he replied that she woke him every day. "But what about weekends," I asked. Doesn't it bother you that she wakes you up on Saturdays and Sundays?"

"No. She never does it on weekends." Jay still doesn't know how she knew the difference.

Kitty passed away at age eighteen after a long and full life. Everyone in our family misses her. And that's quite a legacy for a cat nobody wanted.

Our Green and Silver Surprise

"The quality of mercy is not strained. If falleth as a gentle rain from heaven upon the place beneath. It is twice blessed. It blesses him who gives and him who receives. It is an attribute of God himself."
~ William Shakespeare ~

My mother is not a poker player. Because Mom has a 'tell.' A 'tell' is a facial expression or mannerism that let's the whole world know when you're bluffing. Mom's inability to put on a poker face was very useful to us as children. We always knew when she was hiding something. And so every Christmas we'd pump her for information about our presents.

Dad was keenly aware of Mom's inability to deceive anyone. So he would nip any Christmas questions in the bud. If we asked him, "Is our Christmas present bigger than a bread box?" Dad would invariably answer in Dutch. "Kinderen vragen naar vensterbank." Roughly translated that means, "Children ask at window seats." It's pretty hard to argue with that.

We had a tradition when I was a child. We always bought our Christmas tree on December 20th. December 20th is my mother's birthday. Every year we celebrated at her favourite restaurant and on the way home we'd buy her a tree. There was no point asking Christmas related questions before December 20th, but after that, well, all's fair in love and war and Christmas.

The year I was eight, there was a snowstorm on Mom's birthday. It started in the afternoon with bone-chilling wind gusts and soon there were four-foot drifts. It was obvious that we wouldn't be going out for dinner or a Christmas tree. That December 20th was also the last day of school before our Christmas holiday. After we were dismissed my brother noticed the janitor throwing out the school's magnificent nine-foot Christmas tree. No slouch, he sprinted over and asked if we could have it. The janitor was only too pleased to get rid of it, so Jay and I took turns dragging it home through the snow covered streets of Toronto.

We felt like heroes that snowy afternoon! Mom might not be getting her dinner on the town but she was sure going to have a Christmas tree! Mom was delighted and Dad immediately took the tree to his workshop to trim it down to size. Mom was simply beaming. Not one to miss an opportunity, I casually asked her, "Mom what colour are our Christmas presents this year?"

"Green and silver," she replied temporarily forgetting Dad's interdiction against giving us clues.

"We're getting bikes!" I yelled.

Mom turned three shades of pale.

Jay, a consummate poker player, immediately rushed over to study her face.

"Wha...wha...what makes you...uh...think...it's b...bikes?" she stammered.

"We are getting bikes!" Jay exclaimed.

Then Jay and I began dancing around the living room. "We're getting bikes! We're getting bikes!"

When Dad heard the commotion he came running upstairs. He didn't say a word. He just looked at Mom and then at us. I'll always remember that look. Suddenly we didn't feel like celebrating anymore.

On Christmas morning standing under the Christmas tree there were two brand new green and silver bicycles: quite an extravagance for a family of relatively modest means. How Mom and Dad must have looked forward to giving us those bikes for Christmas! Yet somehow, unintentionally, we stole away much of their joy that Christmas morning. Still, neither one of them mentioned it. They simply forgave us.

"The quality of mercy is not strained...It is twice blessed. It blesses him who gives and him who receives."

Although Dad is gone now, Jay and I still share Mom's birthday dinner every December 20th. Then we put up her tree. But we won't ask her about our presents. It's a question neither of us has asked since the Christmas of our green and silver surprise.

Giving No Quarter

"If you do not forgive others, neither will your Heavenly Father forgive you."
~ Matthew 6:15 ~

There once was an obnoxious old miser who died and found himself at the pearly gates. He was extremely wealthy and wanted first class accommodation in heaven.

St. Peter's assistant was on duty. Glancing at the miser's file, he replied, "I don't see here where you ever forgave anyone or did a good deed. Haven't you ever done anything nice?"

The miser was stumped but then his face lit up. "I once left a waiter a ten cent tip and I gave fifteen cents to the Salvation Army last Christmas."

The assistant picked up the phone, "I'll have to call St. Peter for a ruling."

After he hung up the miser asked, "Well, what did he say?"

"He said, 'Return the old goat's quarter and tell him to go to hell.'"

I loved that joke when I was a kid. Probably because it had a cuss word in it but mostly because it appealed to my sense of justice. The bad guy was always punished and the good guy always triumphed in my comic book world. Yes, everything was black and white when I was nine.

That is until one afternoon when Dad arrived home in a taxi:

"Hey Dad, where's the car?" I inquired.

Dad explained that a tractor-trailer driver had turned too sharply at an intersection and bashed in the front of our Oldsmobile.

A few weeks later Dad got a summons to testify against the truck driver in court. I was thrilled at the chance for retribution. "Boy, I hope he goes to jail!"

Dad wasn't pleased with me. "It's nearly Christmas. I'm sure that man has a family."

The day before the trial, Dad seemed upset - wondering aloud whether the truck driver would lose his license and his livelihood. Dad headed to the car, "Tell your mother I'm going to check something out."

The next evening Dad explained where he'd gone. He'd returned to the accident scene and made an interesting discovery. The road crew had repainted the stop line moving it ten feet back from the intersection. It had obviously been too close for safety on the day of the accident. Dad told the judge all about it at the trial.

The judge seemed impressed, "Mr. Smit, do you think the defendant was at fault?"

"No, Your Honour. Under the circumstances, I think he did the best he could."

"Me too," exclaimed the judge with a flourish. "Case dismissed!"

In my zeal for retribution it never occurred to me the truck driver might be innocent.

The next summer Mom and Dad decided to put a new kitchen floor in the cottage. Dad mentioned it to my elderly Godfather during our usual Sunday visit. Mr. Millen was a lonely old man - his family and friends long gone. He was also having trouble making ends meet on his small pension. So he asked Dad for the job.

Unfortunately, Mr. Millen was no handyman. When he was done, the tiles were crooked and there was tar all over the kitchen. I thought Mr. Millen would apologize. Instead he began yelling at Dad about shoddy materials and uneven floors. Then he stormed out. Dad had to fix the mess himself.

We didn't visit Mr. Millen for the next few weeks but one Sunday afternoon Dad unexpectedly drove into his driveway.

I protested, "But he yelled at you, Dad!"

"That doesn't make any difference."

When he saw us, old Mr. Millen came running outside. Tears were streaming down his face. I never realized before then just how lonely he really was or how much he cherished those Sunday visits.

He offered to return the cheque but Dad refused it, "The job wasn't bad at all – just needed a little cleanup!"

Mr. Millen seemed relieved and after that we never missed another Sunday.

That same year I got my first male teacher: Mr. Bragg. I worshipped the ground he walked on. I still remember an aphorism he taught us: "Never criticize anyone unless you're perfect, but if you were perfect, you wouldn't criticize."

One afternoon he was called out of the classroom. He put us on our honour to be quiet while he was away. The kid behind me immediately started chattering. He prattled on endlessly until I finally turned around and shook my head signaling him to stop. Unfortunately, Mr. Bragg returned at that very moment. He heard talking, saw the back of my head and made a judgment.

"Ray, you disappoint me; I put you on your honour.
"But Mr. Bragg, it wasn't me. Honest!"
"Mr. Smit, you're a liar!"

I was crushed. Despite my pleas, he never forgave me. For the rest of the term he referred to me coldly as, "Hey, you." He transferred that June and I never saw him again. Nonetheless, I'm oddly grateful to him. For though my parents taught me how positive it is to forgive, Mr. Bragg showed me how painful it is - if we don't.

"If you do not forgive others, neither will your Father in Heaven forgive you." Words I try to remember – before someone returns my quarter.

Belling the Hepcat

"Everything is funny as long as it's happening to someone else."
~ Will Rogers ~

As any self-respecting mouse will tell you that no rodent is safe until the cat has been belled.

Everyone has at least one special talent. My brother Jay has many but the most galling is his mastery of practical jokes. Even as a child, Jay's timing and delivery were works of art. And, to his credit, he never debased his gift by using joy buzzers or whoopee cushions. He was way too cool for that. His practical jokes were always elegant - never mean-spirited.

I was a royal pain when we were children: always tagging along and making a nuisance of myself. One evening Dad was invited to the home of an important business contact. Jay quickly made friends with their teenage son, Bill. There was no one my age to play with so I spent my time interrupting. After fifteen minutes, an exasperated Bill suggested that he and Jay head up to the attic for some privacy. As he pulled down the ladder, I began to whine.

"I want to go to."

Jay got a mischievous look on his face. "Oh no, you're much too young to climb the ladder!"

"I am not," I whimpered.

"Well okay, but you're not old enough to go first," Jay replied.

"I am too. I wanna be first!"

Reluctantly Jay and Bill agreed. I proudly climbed the ladder and stepped into the attic. A split second later the ladder disappeared and the attic hatchway slammed shut. It was pitch black. The only sound I could hear was Jay and Bill laughing below me. I'd been bamboozled! Being clear-headed and sensible, I began screaming like a little girl. A few minutes the laughter stopped and the hatchway opened. My Dad was standing at the top of the ladder.

"What on earth do you think you're doing in the Tasker's attic?"

I was so angry I couldn't speak.

Jay, stifling a laugh, said, "Ray, use your words."

"@%$#%@!" I yelled.

"Not those words!" Jay exclaimed.

"Oh, my!" Mrs. Tasker gasped.

Mom blushed. Dad took off his belt and we were hastily on our way home. We weren't invited back.

Jay was by no means the only fellow in his circle good at practical joking. One Saturday night he was visiting his friend Jack in Vancouver. As it neared midnight, they began to get the munchies. Suddenly Jack bolted from his chair and ran outside. Jay looked down from the balcony and saw a pizza delivery driver searching for a house. Jack stopped him, handed him a twenty and bounded upstairs with a pizza.

"Didn't that guy ask you who you were?" Jay inquired.

"No, he just wanted to know if I was there for the pizza. And I was."

About forty minutes later, the driver was back again. An angry middle-aged man came running out of his house and started bellowing, "Thirty minutes my Aunt Fanny. Where the heck were you? What are you a moron?"

Watching from the window, Jay shook his head sadly. "It's so hard to get good help these days!"

"Indeed," Jack replied munching solemnly on the last slice of pizza. "Indeed."

You'd think that when he reached middle age, Jay would have put practical jokes behind him. Not so. Shortly after moving to his townhouse, Jay received a two-week visit from our brother-in-law. Most of Jay's stuff was still in boxes. Since Cam doesn't enjoy cooking, he agreed to do the dishes if Jay would prepare the meals.

Every night after supper, Cam would dutifully start to clean up the enormous stack of dishes. It wasn't until the last night of his visit that he noticed something was amiss. After drying several large colanders he suddenly exclaimed, "Hey wait a minute. You didn't use a colander tonight. Where the heck did these come from?"

"The closet," Jay replied. "Every night since you've been here I've opened a box of dishes. In the last two weeks you've washed every pot, pan and dish I own."

Unlike Cam, Jay found the whole matter inordinately entertaining. I guess Will Rogers was right, "Everything is funny as long as it's happening to someone else."

Being punked by Jay is like a rite of passage in our family. Unfortunately, I've never been able to return the favour. He always wins. Still, I do have one advantage that he doesn't. I have a book. And it might be just a tad more difficult for him to pull one of his patented pranks if people are expecting it.

The hepcat has been belled. Long live the mice.

CHAPTER SIX:

BOTH MY THUMBS ARE BLUE

"Don't ever take a fence down until you know the reason why it was put up."
~ G.K. Chesterton ~

Don't It Turn Your Green Thumb Blue

"If there was a big gardening convention, and you got up and gave a speech in favor of fast-motion gardening, I bet you' would get booed right off the stage. They're just not ready."
~Jack Handey ~

Last spring I decided to try my hand at organic gardening. No more frozen store-bought produce for me. No sir! I was going to self-sufficient: a 'green' gardener if there ever was one.

My sister Femmie once sent me a book on gardening. I leafed through it on Christmas Day so I figured I was pretty much ready for anything.

In early June I picked up a bunch of starter plants at the hardware store and set to planting. I fully expected dozens of jealous neighbours would soon be dropping by asking for advice.

"Ray. How did you grow such big tomatoes?"

"Rinse, lather and repeat. Always remember to repeat."

"Mr. Smit," a young lad would say tugging his forelock, "my Dad says you're the Ned Flanders of horticulture."

"Golly gee willikers thanks, son. What's your question?"

"Mr. Smit, will you teach us to garden?"

"When you children are old enough you can take my college course: Gardening 101. Until then you don't have to call me Mr. Smit. I'm a humble man. Just call me Professor Ray."

"What will we learn, Professor Ray?"

"Firstly, you'll learn how to pasteurize. That's the method gardeners use to kill insects in their pastures. Then we'll cover germination. That's how we rid our gardens of germs and other harmful viruses. You'll learn about the history of gardening and about the two greatest gardeners who ever lived: Pete Moss and Beau Tanicle. And finally, as a class project we'll take pictures of everything you grow: that's what we call photosynthesis."

I was happily daydreaming about my new college career when Jay arrived. His first question was, "Did you prepare the soil?"

"You bet. I watered it this morning."

"No I mean did you fertilize?"

"Please there are children present!"

"Do you know how to spread manure?"

"Obviously you haven't read my column recently."

"Very funny. But did you add manure before planting your vegetables?"

"Don't be gross!"

"Plants need manure to grow."

"I'm not eating anything that's grown in …well never mind."

"What kind of tomatoes did you plant?"

"Big juicy ones."

My brother inspected the plants. "These are Roma tomatoes."

"Yes they do smell good."

"No they're called 'Romas' not 'Aromas' and they're very small."

"They won't be small when I'm done with them."

"You should plant Beefsteak tomatoes"

"I don't eat beef."

"Oh, never mind." My brother shrugged his shoulders and left - no doubt intimidated by my superior knowledge of gardening.

Several weeks later harvest began. I brought some tomatoes over for Mom.

"Look!" she said to my stepfather Henry. "Ray brought us some prunes."

"Those are tomatoes," I protested.

"But they're all wrinkled and purple. No, these are prunes."

Henry began to chortle. "Maybe they're olives. Let's press them and use the olive oil on our salad - if we only had some tomatoes."

"Very funny!" I replied.

"Look, Mom, I also brought over some yellow beans for you guys - a whole bag full. Mom looked at them curiously and then snapped one.

"Actually I don't think these are yellow beans."

"Then why are they yellow?" I asked cleverly.

"Good question. I think they used to be green…"

Next year maybe I'll pick them a little earlier.

The following day with wounded pride I went to the grocery store and got a whole bunch of fresh veggies, which I delivered to my folks in a plain paper bag.

"So you don't think I can grow vegetables, hmmm? Well then what do you think of these?"

Mom was impressed. She then added the coupe de grace. "They're wonderful - and how clever of you to make your own 'Grown in BC' stickers just like the ones in the store!"

Well not all dreams come true. I won't be teaching a college course in agriculture anytime soon. But I'm still a green gardener. Yes, sir, very green, indeed.

CALL ME GILLIGAN

"If at first you don't succeed, try, try again. Then give up."
~ W.C. Fields ~

As I've mentioned once or twice before, my brother Jay is one of those guys who can build anything. Give him five rusty screws and a 2x4 and he'll create a stereo stand. Add in a couple of ragged shards of metal and he'll build an antique desk. With the same materials I could build five rusty screws, a 2x4 and some ragged shards of metal. If we were stuck on Gilligan's Island he'd be the Skipper and I'd be Gilligan.

My lack of manly technical skills has long been a source of worry for my brother. A few years back, he decided it was high time I learned the fundamentals of carpentry. Coincidentally he'd also just bought a fixer-upper in the country and needed an assistant.

I caught wind of Jay's plans on Christmas Day when my presents were a genuine leather tool belt and a brand new Black and Decker reversible drill. Although I would have preferred golf clubs, I attempted to get into the spirit of his gifts. I tried on the tool belt and put the drill in the holster. As I checked my look in the mirror I grabbed my cowboy hat - Alberta ladies love cowboys - and practiced pulling the drill out of the holster. I got pretty good at it too except for the four-inch scratch I put into the bathtub. But I bet even the Billy the Kid had the occasional bathroom accident. After all he was just a child.

Without doubt, I was the spitting image of Robert Redford in *Butch Cassidy and the Sundance Kid*! But when I stomped out of the bathroom, I was met with gales of laughter.

"You look like Hoss Cartwright from *Bonanza*," my mother giggled.

"You look ridiculous," my brother concluded.

Suitably crestfallen I returned to the mirror. I had to admit that at 250 pounds I probably wasn't the spitting image of Sundance. But Hoss wasn't so bad. He may never have gotten the girl, but he sure could handle a six-shooter.

Early the next Saturday morning, I arrived at my brother's new western abode and was given the grand tour. There were sticky doors, leaky pipes and drywall that needed sanding and painting. I ran out to the car to retrieve my toolbox. This looked like it might be fun. I figured I'd pick up a few tips from my older brother and in no time I'd be building fences and gazebos and maybe even a log cabin in the mountains. And even though I'd long ago given up the idea of having my own TV show, perhaps Bob Vila would have me on his program as a guest:

"What kind of nails did you use, Ray? Were they four inch Edsels?"

"Heck, no. A frontiersman doesn't buy nails. He forges his own.

"Did you have any trouble with the plumbing?"

"No. Once you get past the intubation process, it's a simple matter of osculating the joiners and lactating the pump."

"My friend, the swimsuit model, would like you to fix the doorjamb in her apartment and then maybe stay for a late supper."

"I'll get my cowboy hat and head right over."

I was given some very serious thought as to how I'd fix a sticky doorjamb when I heard a loud, "Ahem," behind me. It was Jay inquiring if I was planning to do any actual work that day. Hitching up my belt I asked, "Well now what shall I start with? The doorjambs? The plumbing?"

My brother seemed amused. " No," he said. "You have to walk before you run." He then pulled out a sanding block and several sheets of sandpaper. He smiled and said, "Have fun - you'll be sanding all the walls so they'll be ready for painting." After several hours, I knew how Ralph Macchio felt in the *Karate Kid* movies. "Wax on…wax off, Daniel San. Wax on…wax off."

My tool tutelage ended on the exact day my brother's house was finished. I never did get to operate my new Black and Decker reversible drill. Nor did I get to use my tool belt, although it was a wonderful place to store Milky Way bars. I sure as heck never learned how to build a log cabin or fix a swimsuit model's doorjamb. W.C. Fields was right. "If at first you don't succeed, try, try again. Then give up."

It also pays to beware of brothers bearing gifts.

Awl's Well That Ends Well

"Hard work never killed anybody, but why take a chance?"
~ Edgar Bergen ~

My father lived the protestant work ethic. He always said, "You can accomplish anything if you set your mind to it. All that's required is hard work!"

When we were young, Dad's constant emphasis on work was difficult to comprehend. Mom tried to help us understand his single-mindedness by telling us stories about his life in Holland during the war. She told us that food was scarce so Dad would moonlight every Saturday at some local farm. For 12 hours of backbreaking labour he'd receive some eggs or a sack of vegetables. And to his credit, his family never went hungry.

Mom's favourite story was about a nasty old farmer's wife in North Holland. She was especially abusive to farmhands. One Saturday after 8 hours in the fields, Dad was sent to the house. There were several gallons of cream that needed to be churned. Unfortunately four hours of churning produced no butter at all. The farmer's wife was incensed!

"No money for you," she said in a pique of temper. "I'll give you some cream but no pay!" She poured it into two huge leather bags and sent him on his way. Dad could barely carry the two cream-laden bags outside let alone pedal his bike with its wooden wheels. He must have been a comical sight on the way home, barely able to pedal with the bags swaying violently from side to side.

He arrived home late and crestfallen. But something unexpected happened during the bumpy ride home. When Dad opened the bags, the cream had turned to butter! Enough for several expensive one-pound bricks! And even though the farmer's wife was a conniving, nasty, mean-spirited old harridan, Mom maintains to this day that she and Dad liked her just fine that night!

As I grew older I genuinely wanted to live up to my Dad's work ethic. He, however, had his doubts about me.

One summer Dad paid a man two hundred dollars to cut down several dead elm trees that were overhanging our cottage. There were several stumps left over which the tree-cutter offered to remove for another fifty. Dad was incredulous. Pay money to remove perfectly good firewood? Was he kidding? The tree-cutter told him that dead elm is impossible to cut up without a heavy-duty chainsaw. "Don't need a chainsaw. My son will take care of it." Dad replied giving me a knowing grin. "He isn't afraid of a little hard work!"

I knew somehow that this was a test and I was determined to pass it. I placed the awl in the middle of a stump and started swinging Dad's sledgehammer for dear life. After about 20 minutes, the awl was an inch below the stump's surface but there wasn't a crack in sight.

Dad was ticked. "You know what awls cost?" Here use another one and this time do it right! Several minutes later the other one disappeared too. Dad was choked. "How often have I told you? You can accomplish anything in this life. If you work hard enough!"

Dad drove up to the hardware store and bought four wedges and three awls. When he returned he grabbed the sledgehammer and sent me inside to help my mother. When I came outside later the stump still wasn't split. It did, however, contain four wedges, five awls, a tomahawk and my Dad's brand new axe-blade. The handle was now in the lake. He stared out at the water for several minutes and finally said, "Next week maybe we'll buy a chain saw. Now let's go home." Neither of us mentioned it again but it was the last time he ever questioned my work ethic.

I still believe in the values that my father taught me: "You can accomplish anything that you set your mind to it! All that's required is hard work."

It also helps to have a chainsaw.

Frank Lloyd Wrong

"There's more than one way to skin a cat."
~ Ancient Proverb ~

Shortly after I bought my first house, Jay came over to help me fix it up. As usual, I was the gopher while Jay worked his magic installing new doors and windows.

"I wish I could find a trade that suited me," I sighed.

"You're a writer."

"No, I mean something macho like welding or hair styling."

"Hair styling?"

"Worked for Warren Beatty."

"Well maybe you could try something artistic like wallpapering."

"You mean I could be an interior decorator like Frank Lloyd Wright?"

"He was an architect."

"Yes and also a fine interior decorator."

"Not really."

"That's a great idea. What's more macho than interior decorating?"

"Hairstyling?"

"Never mind."

That afternoon I picked out a particularly vibrant tartan pattern – it was the only one on sale for some reason- and headed home to start my new career. I ignored the instructions – after all I was now a professional decorator. In a half-hour I was already finished. Nothing to it! I went outside with a coffee and checked my tomato plants. They were dead. No matter. I was a decorator not a farmer.

When I came back inside there were air pockets the size of balloons along the walls. Not a problem for an expert. I just pricked the holes in each balloon and glued the paper back down with bulldog grip.

Later that evening Jay popped by.

"Impressed?" I asked smugly.

"No. Nauseous," he replied. "Tartan is an accent. You don't wallpaper a whole room with it."

"Oh," I replied sheepishly.

"Better take it down," he said tugging on a corner.

A quarter inch came off in his hand. He glared at me. "Did you buy strippable wallpaper?"

"Of course," I replied, unsure of what he meant. "Do you think I'm an idiot?"

There was a long silence. But I'm sure we both knew the answer. Still, it took the better part of a week and three putty knives to take it all back down.

A few years later I moved to Qualicum Beach and Jay invited me to stay with him until I found a house. One night after supper, Jay was napping when I went into the bathroom to wash my hands. The cat followed me in to use the litter box. She'd had Boston bluefish for supper. And whenever she ate bluefish, things began happening in her entrails - evil, unspeakable things. I made a mad dash for the door wondering if I should make an emergency call to the Ministry of the Environment.

A few seconds later the cat smugly strolled out of the bathroom and gave me a smirk. Unfortunately, all the commotion woke Jay up. When Kitty heard him getting out of bed she took off for the living room. I was still standing there holding a wet towel and my breath when he opened his bedroom door.

"Sweet merciful heavens," he exclaimed. "Go visit a doctor!"

"But it wasn't me. It was the cat. Boston bluefish doesn't agree with her."

"Oh, that's the saddest cop-out I've ever heard. Blaming a poor defenseless cat. At least you could have opened the window."

"But, it wasn't me, it was the cat!"

Jay headed to the living room only to find Kitty curled up on the couch. "Blaming a innocent sleeping cat. That's just pathetic."

Kitty purred sweetly as Jay went to the kitchen to get her royal innocence a treat. As soon as he was gone, she shot me a haughty look.

"Someday," I muttered.

Jay spent that summer remodeling the house. Everything was done except the bathroom so, when Jay took a trip to Alberta, I decided to redecorate it for him. I bought the most expensive wallpaper I could find. It looked just like the foil wrap he bought every Christmas, so I knew he'd love it. This time I followed all of the instructions and the paper actually stayed on the wall. Not a single balloon.

When Jay got home he was dumbstruck. "My bathroom looks like it was decorated by Santa Claus."

"Thank you," I enthused.

"I think the stripes are supposed to be vertical not horizontal."

"Well you said I should explore my artistic side."

"I think I'm developing vertigo."

"Must be the long car trip."

The next evening, Jay had a hankering for his favourite: Boston bluefish. As we sat down to dinner, I had an idea. I surreptiously slipped Kitty all the fish she could swallow and waited for nature to take its course. As we started our desserts, Kitty headed down the hall and began making loud scratching noises in the litter box.

I waited. A few seconds later Jay rushed to open a window. Meanwhile, the cat ambled back into the kitchen. Jay looked at her with disgust.

"Man! Kitty, you stink!"

Kitty shot me a dirty look. I responded with an innocent smile.

"You smell," Jay repeated accusingly.

Kitty turned haughtily and sauntered back down the hall.

"What? Can't take a little constructive criticism?" I remarked under my breath. Meanwhile Jay spent several minutes spraying air freshener and issuing dark threats about the cat's diet.

Later, as Jay took the litter box outside, I admired his bathroom décor with quiet satisfaction. Not a bad result all around, I thought. Even if I wasn't another Frank Lloyd Wright.

WOULD YOU LIKE A TRIM?

"Don't ask the barber whether you need a haircut."
~ Daniel Greenburg ~

When I was seven, I hated getting my haircut. Still do. So when Dad started making noises about a trip to the barbershop, I decided to take matters into my own hands. Yes sir, a few minutes of expert trimming and Dad was certain to recant and forget all about the barbershop. I grabbed the scissors and started cutting my bangs. Unfortunately, I cut hair with the same precision that I cut wood. When I was done, my bangs hung at a 45-degree angle and one sideburn was about two inches higher than the other. Years later that style would be called the asymmetrical cut. My father called it a disaster and took me straight to Clem the barber.

Old Clem was not impressed. For the next ten minutes as he clipped and snipped the mess I'd made, he got more and more irritated. Finally snarling in total frustration he took out the clippers and let them do their work. I was totally intimidated.

"Who gave you that stupid haircut, kid?"

"My mom," I lied shamelessly.

When Mom came to pick me up, Clem had a thing or two to tell her about her lack of proficiency with the scissors.

Mom said nothing to Clem but did have a few choice words for me about lying on the way home in the car. Still, she didn't impose a punishment - no doubt deciding my new haircut was punishment enough.

Last year knowing that it would be a busy summer, I decided something short was in order. I briefly thought of doing the job myself - but even though it was forty years later I was still afraid I might botch the job and run into Clem at the barbershop. "Who gave you that stupid haircut, kid?" I knew even Clem wouldn't believe me now it if I blamed my mom. So I decided to visit a stylist instead.

It had been quite a while since my last adventure in the barbers' chair. I was beginning to look like a cross between an Irish setter and Harpo Marx. Elderly women were making wide circles around me muttering, "dirty hippie," under their breath. Children looked at me like I was some kind of museum piece.

"Daddy, is that what the flower children looked like in

the sixties?"

"Just the middle-aged ones, son."

My brain turns to mush as soon as I walk into a barbershop. I just want it over with as soon as possible so I'll agree to almost anything.

The stylist greeted me with, "So I guess you haven't had a haircut in quite a while have you?" As she surveyed the stringy mop on top of my head, she asked sweetly, "What on earth are we going to do with this?"

I managed to mutter, "I'd like something shorter for the summer?"

"Really, really short, right?"

"Um. Uh sure if you think so," I agreed nervously. She smiled and picked up the clippers. After a few minutes of loud buzzing, I was headed out the door. For some reason the theme song from *Kojack* kept running through my head.

Making fun of someone's haircut is the last vestige of politically incorrect humour. You can't attack someone's religion, race or nationality and rightly so. But just dare to get an unflattering haircut and it's open season:

My brother stared at me for a minute and then started laughing. "Look, it's Mr. Clean!"

I was late for the airport or I would have said something brilliant in repose. When I got to the arrival gate, my friend Sal was just getting his bag. He took one look at me and started to chuckle. "Do you have any literature for me to read?"

"What do you mean?"

"Aren't you going to chant Hare Krishna and ask me for money?"

It's amazing how many bad jokes there are about haircuts. And my friends seemingly knew them all. The only thing missing was a rim shot.

"Better put a hat on the head, son. There's a woodpecker convention in town."

Barum Pum!

"Too bad you don't have three holes in your head. Because I sure need a new bowling ball."

Kating Ding!

Or my personal favourite. "Hey Ray. When did you get your head circumcised?"

Although it seemed like an eternity, I survived the summer and eventually my hair grew back. Last week I went for another summer haircut but I was determined not to be cannon fodder for any more jokes. As I sat down in the barber's chair, the stylist picked up the clippers and said, "Summer haircut? I think it'd look better really short."

Incomprehensibly, I replied, "Whatever you think." All the while wondering if her name was Clementine.

If anyone's looking for me, I'll be at the airport. All I need's a tambourine and a robe. With a little luck I'll raise enough money for a new hat.

CHAPTER SEVEN:

IF LIFE GIVES YOU LEMONS, PUCKER UP.

"My luck is so bad that if I bought a cemetery, people would stop dying."
~ Rodney Dangerfield ~

FebruWary

"Blow, blow thou winter wind."
~William Shakespeare~

I hate February. If the rainy days and frigid nights weren't enough, the insipid traditions make it nearly unbearable:

The month starts off with a celebration of rats. Oh sure, we call them cute names like groundhogs and woodchucks, but essentially they're enormous rats. Every February 2nd we prod and poke them until they grudgingly give us free meteorological advice. And what do we get for our efforts? Six more weeks of winter and twenty-six more days of February. If it were any other month we'd call pest control instead.

Next comes an exercise in futility called Valentine's Day. It is a loathsome celebration created to humiliate single guys named Ray. This year's celebration was the cruelest ever. I'd given up hope of getting a Valentine when one appeared on my email just before midnight. When I opened it, all it said was:

"Happy Valentine's Day, Ray. You're a SWEATY."

A 'sweaty?'

Jay looked at it and laughed, "Maybe she thinks you're going through the change."

"Are you implying I'm not macho?"

"No, I'm not *implying*..."

I walked by the hall mirror and stopped. "Maybe I do have a wrinkle or two I should get rid of."

"Have you considered a sandblaster?"

"Very funny. They say cucumbers can reduce the bags under your eyes."

"How about a watermelon?"

"Some women use Preparation H."

"Yes the perfect trifecta for your imaginary Valentine's date: shower, shave and hemorrhoids."

The other miserable thing about this time of year is its effect on my waistline. Each and every February I gain enough weight to resemble the Michelin Man. Although, to be fair, it's not really my fault. National Pistachio Day, National Tortilla Chip Day, National Chocolate Mint Day and National Sticky Bun Day are all in February. And being patriotic, I have to do my best to support them. I guess it's no small wonder that February 9th is National Toothache Day.

Because I'm middle-aged, certain physical changes are becoming noticeable in my life. But why do they always present themselves in February? Recently, I developed some artery problems with the unfortunate side effect that the hair on my legs is disappearing at an alarming rate. Naturally, I mentioned it to my doctor. He gave me a bemused look and asked if I'd like a transplant or a toupee? And they say laughter is the best medicine!

Most people are like me. They know how horrible February is. That's why it's only 28 days long. Except, of course, during leap year when there's that stupid, superfluous 29th day. Now who's the moron who decided that? If you have to add a leap year day, why do it in February? Why not have a July 32nd? Now that's a day I could look forward to once every four years – although I probably wouldn't wear shorts.

Strangely, this year I'd nearly made a tepid peace with February - that is until Nan, one of the nurses at Mom's care home, Chrysanthemum Lodge, stopped me in the hallway.

"Hey, Ray. Guess what? I saw your picture in the paper?"

"You did? That's great!"

I immediately wondered if the editor had put my column on the front page where it belongs. Or maybe I'd won some kind of literary award. Perhaps February wasn't such a bad month after all.

"Where was my picture, Nan?" I asked exultantly.

"In the aviary. I was feeding my budgies, when I noticed one of your old columns was lining the bottom of the birdcage."

"Oh."

"Yes, and when I said 'Look, Budgie, there's Ray's picture,' the cutest thing happened."

"Really?"

"Yup, she dropped a load smack dab in the middle of your photo."

Small wonder they're not called lovebirds.

I guess Shakespeare was right. 'Blow, blow thou

winter wind' and take this foul month with you. As for me, the only day I'll be celebrating this February is the 28th - Public Sleeping Day. I'll be pulling the covers over my head and counting the hours until this accursed month is finally over.

Until then be FebruWary!

There's No Fool Like An April Fool

"Without fools the rest of us could not succeed."
~ *Mark Twain* ~

I detest the first of April. Every year on April Fool's Day someone or something makes me look ridiculous. It's only a question of how.

One March afternoon when I was a nine, our phone quit. While I was watching the repairman fix it, he dialed some numbers and made it ring! Fascinated I asked him the secret and he wrote down the magic equation. Early on April 1st, I dialed those numbers, disguised my voice and waited for Mom to answer the extension.

"Hello, this is Mr. Pilke, the principal," I intoned.

"Hello, Mr. Pilke," my mom replied.

"I called to tell you that today is a holiday, Mom... I mean Mrs. Smit."

"How nice of you to call. It's a little surprising since you retired last year."

"He did? Err...I mean, yes I did."

"Congratulations. By the way, how's your wife. What's her name, again?"

"I forget."

"But you won't forget to go to school today, will you Ray?

"No Ma'am."

I tried the phone bit every April Fool's Day. It never worked...It still doesn't.

I especially remember one April 1st when I was in Grade 10. My history teacher arrived in a particularly foul mood:

"We're having a pop quiz today. It will constitute 75% of your final grade." Then he went to the board and wrote the following words: *Agriculture, Politics, Religion, Industry, Land, Food, Organization, Oracles, Legislature* and *Science."*

"I want 500 words on each topic as it relates to Greek history."

Then, to our horror, he began to wipe off the board. Luckily, he left the first letter of each word and sat down. What was left? A-P-R-I-L-F-O-O-L-S.

It was hilarious. True, 68% of the class went on to become chronically incontinent ...but I digress.

A few years ago, just before April Fool's Day, I began having an irregular heartbeat. I lived in a mining town and was sent directly to the lab. A stern older woman was in charge.

"I'm here for irregularity."

"Try bran. Next!"

"No, I'm here for a halter top," I whispered conspiratorially.

"A halter top?" she exclaimed in a voice loud enough to wake Jimmy Hoffa. "Have you tried the softer side of Sears?"

Several miners were laughing as I tried to regain my composure.

"My doctor wants me to wear a halter top," I practically yelled in frustration.

"Well, it's none of my business what two consenting adults…."

"No. It's for an irregular heartbeat. I'm supposed to get a halter."

"Oh you mean a *Holter* monitor. Have a seat."

A few minutes later she glued a bunch of electrodes to my chest, stuck a tape recorder on my belt and sent me home. Luckily, everything was fine.

A few years later, I was sent for another Holter test. I wasn't worried about looking foolish until I entered the exam room. There was a razor on the table.

"What's that for?" I asked the nice lab technician.

"I'm going to shave your chest."

A few minutes later I felt like a plucked chicken. Looking in the mirror, I quickly regretted gaining those extra middle-age pounds. I was perplexed to see what had developed – so to speak.

After the electrodes were attached, I grabbed for my shirt. But before I could, the lab tech handed me a fishnet stocking.

"I have big feet. This will never fit."

"Actually, it goes over your head."

After much tugging and pulling she managed to get it over my shoulders. Predictably, it was so snug in some places; it caused me to protrude in others. Places where a guy shouldn't protrude! Worse still, the radio was playing, *Man, I feel Like A Woman.*

"I look ridiculous," I complained dispiritedly.

"Perhaps you could try a few piercings and a tattoo," she laughed.

I doubt it. It's hard to look punk when you have more rolls than the Coombs bakery.

Luckily, my test results were normal. On the other hand, ever since my plucking I've had an irrational fear of corsets. Like I said, I detest April Fool's Day because I always end up looking ridiculous. I guess Twain was right, "Without fools the rest of us could not succeed."

No need to thank me.

Stick to the Accordion

"A bachelor is a souvenir of some woman who found a better one at the last minute."
~ Anonymous ~

People often wonder why I'm still single. There is no easy answer to that question.

When I was little, I lived and breathed hockey. I had two goals in life: to play center for the Toronto Maple Leafs and to impress Jo-Anne Cutter, the cutest girl in grade four. I was – at the risk of repeating myself - the best road hockey player on my street. I had the hardest shot, the best deek and the most speed. In fact, I fancied myself a prodigy much like the great Bobby Orr.

Of course, excelling at road hockey wasn't enough. After a while I wanted to play in the big leagues: the Metro Toronto Minor Hockey Association. And when I was nine, Mom and Dad finally relented and signed me up. We went down to the skate exchange and Dad picked out a pair of used skates for me. They were easily two sizes too big but Dad said I'd grow into them.

"No point, having to buy new skates every year. Just wear a couple of extra pairs of socks. Besides these ones are on sale."

When I was nine I was already wearing a size eight men's shoe. So when Mom taught me to dance, I looked like a Clydesdale with a charley horse. Except Clyde probably had a better sense of rhythm. Anyway, off I went to my first game - an overconfident nine year-old wearing size ten men's skates and an assortment of used equipment. My friends from the block were excited to see me given my legendary road hockey status.

"Ray's here! We're gonna have a great team."

"Well boys, I don't mean to brag but I think we'll do alright!"

"Hey, Ray that American kid from down the street is playing too!"

"Oh no, he's awful! He's such a doofus!"

"Yeah, he's a doofus!"

"Don't worry boys, we'll show him how to play the game."

The coach herded us together and told us to head out for the pre-game skate. I furtively hoped that the beautiful Jo-Anne Cutter would be in the stands so I could dazzle her with stick handling and win her heart with my slap shot. But as it turned out she was at ballet class. The

American kid went on the ice first. He was a lousy skater and I groaned as he jiggled up toward center ice.

"Doofus!"

I was the last one on to step onto the rink. "Look out Daryl Sittler. Watch out Gordie Howe."

As I took my first glide, I was suddenly looking up at the clock. I tried to get up but went right back down again.

The American kid skated by and said, "You left your skate guards on...Doofus!"

Embarrassed, I quickly pulled off the smooth white plastic guards and got to my feet. Unfortunately, the removal of the skate guards didn't improve the situation much and I was soon gazing at the clock again. The referee skated by, sighed, picked me up and helped me get to the players bench. As he skated away, I heard him say, 'Doofus.' Must have been referring to that snotty American kid.

As the season progressed it was clear that I was not going to be the next Phil Esposito. It just never occurred to me that I should learn to skate before joining a hockey team. Dad was nonplussed by my lack of ability and totally irritated by the number of early morning practices. Finally, one day after another monotonous pre-dawn exercise in futility he loudly asked me if hockey was really my calling or if I didn't want to try something else.

My friend Steve piped up, "How about ballet dancing?"

I should have slugged him.

Anyway, by the time I was eleven I knew that I'd never be a hockey star. I'd have to find another way to win the fair Jo-Anne's heart. That's when I discovered my real passion - music.

"Dad, I wanna be a rock star just like Mick Jagger and John Lennon."

"What?"

"Dad can I have a guitar?"

"We'll see."

A few weeks later, Dad arrived home with a surprise. "So you wanna play music? Here you go," he said handing me a large suitcase.

"How do you get a guitar in here?" I asked

"Open it."

It was an accordion.

"You learn to play that. Oh yes, and go get a haircut. You can be a musician but I don't want you looking like one of those longhaired Beatles. I hear they get sore throats with all that singing about revolutions and such."

So picture it if you will. An eleven-year-old boy with enormous feet, short hair and no rhythm trying to impress the cutest girl in school with his accordion.

I didn't stand a chance.

"A bachelor is a souvenir of some woman who found a better one at the last minute."

Jo-Anne could hardly miss.

I'm Not Getting Older, I'm Getting Wetter

*"Grow old along with me
The best is yet to be."*
~ John Lennon ~

It's strange how many people fear aging. Not me. I'm not old. I'm just a little ripe.

Where does our dread of aging come from? Primarily, it's cultural. North Americans and Western Europeans are the only people on earth who revere the young instead of the old. In China, one stands when an elderly person enters the room. In Hebraic culture one "honours their father and mother." And contrary to North American films, Eskimos do not put their elderly relatives on ice floes and send them off to die. In fact, almost every other culture of the world reveres the aged and heeds their wise counsel. But not us. More people will listen to an empty-headed swimsuit model than to Al Gore. What the heck does she know about global warming? Although to be fair, Al probably shouldn't be strutting the catwalk in a Speedo either.

Which leads me to my next point. Most of us worry that we'll lose our sexual allure as we age. That's not necessarily true. Paul Newman, Cary Grant, Ray Smit and Clark Gable were all sex symbols well into middle age.

Okay, maybe three out of four. But Ally Sheedy and Meg Ryan are plenty beautiful even though they're not exactly teenagers. And Mae West was still making hearts flutter at eighty!

Some of us fear that if we haven't become famous or successful by the age of fifty, we never will. Balderdash. Grandma Moses practically invented folk art in her seventies and lived to be one hundred and one. Imagine what the world would have lost if she'd settled for prunes and bingo. And let's not forget my personal favourite: Harland Sanders. The colonel was a dismal failure until late in life when he happened upon a particularly yummy chicken recipe. You, of course, know his invention as Kentucky Fried Chicken. I know it as one of the four basic food groups.

Our physical prowess is thought to peak at age eighteen. But is that true? Take Johnny Bower, for instance. Johnny was a second-rate hockey goalie who spent nearly twenty years in the minor leagues. Most sensible people would have given up and taken a real job. Not Johnny. He never quit. He was already in his mid-thirties when Punch Imlach gave him a shot at the NHL. He won four Stanley Cups in the next eleven years. He even went on to record a hit song called, 'Honkey the Christmas Goose.' Not bad for an old guy who should have retired.

And even if you've found a measure of success before middle age, that doesn't mean it's all downhill from there. Consider George Burns. His best days as a comedian were in his nineties. And he wasn't afraid to make fun of his age:

One time he alleged, "When I was a boy the Dead Sea was only sick."

Asked why he went out with young models he replied, "I would go out with women my age, but there are no women my age."

When he was in his sixties, George's physician told him to give up cigars. As he approached one hundred, a reporter asked what the doctor had to say about it now. Burns replied, "I don't know. He's dead!"

Red Skelton also performed well into his eighties. His take on marriage was priceless:

"I married Miss Right. I just didn't know her first name was Always."

"I asked my wife where she wanted to go for our anniversary. 'Somewhere I haven't been in a long time!' she replied. So I suggested the kitchen."

Speaking of food, a good friend of mine recently invited me out to a restaurant.

"I'll be there with bells on. If it's cold, I'll where something warmer." I giggled.

She answered brightly, "There's more of me these days, so I guess there'll more places to hang bells."

I replied, "Gaining weight is a lot like buying real estate. It all depends on location, location, location."

Of course, growing older isn't all parties and fame. Some aspects of aging are challenging - like the aforementioned weight gain. My waist used to be a size 32. I now look like I swallowed an inner tube. People keep asking me if I'm in my third trimester.

And the plumbing doesn't work quite as well as it used to either. When we were teenagers the stream was like a fire hydrant. In our thirties it was like a garden hose. Now it's got all the pressure of a leaky faucet. I feel fortunate at the end of the day if my shoes are dry.

Luckily for me, I'm aging extremely well. I know that because recently at a nursing home a lovely octogenarian told me I was handsome. When she was out of earshot, I vainly repeated, "Handsome. That woman said I was handsome!" Another visitor walking by looked me up and down and whispered, "She must have dementia!"

Notwithstanding evidence to the contrary, aging isn't so bad. "Grow old along with me. The best is yet to be."

That's what I believe. But then I'm not old. I'm just a little ripe.

NOT PRETTY IN PINK

"A man's gotta do what a man's gotta do."
---John Wayne---

"I need new blouses."

My blood ran cold.

Mom doesn't shop anymore. These days she asks her children to buy her clothes. Because my sisters live clear across the country, that task has fallen to me.

"I think your blouses look great, Mom." I replied disingenuously.

"And some pajamas too," she replied, ignoring my protestations. "Something snuggly."

"Snuggly?"

You can send me out for beer or a jackhammer or even a bag of manure, but by all that is good and beautiful please don't send me for something "snuggly."

I once fought off two snarling Rottweilers with my bare hands on a Calgary street. It's true. But those dogs couldn't engender the same level of fear as those two infamous words: 'Ladies Apparel.'

Apprehensively, I headed down to the mall with my brother Jay in tow. We entered a department store where he quickly abandoned me for the hardware department. I hesitantly stood at the edge of the ladies department waiting for some PJ's and a blouse to jump into my cart. I was furtively touching a jacket when a saleslady began eyeing me suspiciously.

"Do you need some help?

"Yes," I whispered, "I need some pajamas."

"Oh really?" She gave me a knowing smile.

"Nothing too frilly."

"Of course. Not every man wants to wear black lace…"

"No, you misunderstand. They have to be snuggly." I felt my face flush.

"Snuggly? Oh dear, in your size that might present a problem."

"No, they're for my Mom."

"Yes, of course they are," she replied with a wink. "They're just behind the accessories."

I strode over, in a very manly way I might add, and grabbed the first two pairs I saw. Then I bid a hasty retreat to the electronics department.

A few minutes later my brother found me. Did you get Mom's blouses?"

"No but I got her pajamas."

"Fine, go get her blouses and we'll be done."

"I don't wanna shop for blouses," I mumbled, helplessly staring at the floor. Exasperated he said, "Oh come on, I'll help you."

We entered the ladies department and Jay headed for the designer clothes. I stood in the corner inconspicuously fingering some rather large blouses and bed jackets. I happened to look in a full-length mirror and noted that my midsection was extending quite a ways beyond my belt. As I beheld myself in profile, two women walked by and started to laugh. I wondered why when I happened to look up. There was a sign that said, 'Maternity Clothes.'

I sucked in my gut and waddled over to the designer section.

Thankfully, Jay had already found two blouses and was getting ready to leave.

"I bet Mom will like these!" I enthused.

"Let's see how they look," my brother teased. Then he took a frilly blouse and jokingly held it up for me to model. "Nope. You're definitely not pretty in pink."

A woman walking by gave me a dirty look.

On the way to the cashier, Jay said, "It's no wonder women take so long to shop. Look at how expensive ladies' clothes are. I could buy a pair of jeans and a two shirts for just one blouse."

Regaining my equilibrium I related Ilie Nastase's famous quote. "I haven't reported my missing credit card to the police because whoever stole it is spending less than my wife."

I was beginning to feel less embarrassed as we reached the cashier. I boldly handed her the PJ's and blouses. She smiled and said, "If you'd like to try these on you'll have to use the men's fitting room not the ladies."

I sputtered, "But they're not for me."

"I understand. You can always try them on at home, dear. Just keep the receipt."

Meanwhile an attractive woman walked up behind us.

Jay smiled at her and said, "I'm buying clothes for my Mom, she's elderly."

"Aren't you the sweetest thing," she replied gushing like Old Faithful! "It's not every man who's that secure."

"I do what I can." Jay replied modestly as I paid the bill.

On the way home, Jay gave me that pitying older brother look and said, "Sometimes, little brother, you're a black hole."

"A black hole?"

"Yes, an incredibly dense phenomenon."

"What do you mean?"

" I mean this: You're single. You're looking to meet nice women. Well, who do women love? Men with babies, puppies or elderly Moms. You just don't know how to take advantage of an opportunity do you?"

He had a point.

Last night when I dropped by to see Mom she said, "Ray, I need some new underwear."

Normally those words would have sent a chill down my spine. Instead I thought of Jay's advice. This was an opportunity!

So if some Saturday, when you see me looking through the black lace panties and push-up bras at Sears, don't get the wrong idea. I'm not a weirdo. I'm just a normal guy taking advantage of an opportunity. Yes sir, 'A man's gotta do, what a man's gotta do.'

John Wayne would be proud!

CHAPTER EIGHT:

PUT UP OR SHUT UP

"Wise men don't need advice. Fools won't take it."
~ Benjamin Franklin ~

A Crust of Dread, A Jug of Whine and Bow-Wow

"The best-laid plans of mice and men often go awry."
~ Robert Burns ~

My mother was an excellent cook. Her meatballs were so amazing I'd choose them over steak anytime. Her potato salad is legendary and I have friends living afar who still rave about her chicken soup - twenty years after eating it.

One evening when I was thirteen, Mom announced she was making pies after supper. My brother and I quickly gathered in the kitchen to watch and wait.

Mom had everything prepared when she opened the cupboard. It was then that she had an 'oh no second.' An 'oh no second' is defined as that exact moment in time you slam the car door and realize you've locked the keys inside. (Parenthetically, it shouldn't be confused with an

'Ono second' which was the exact moment in 1969 when John Lennon married the lovely Miss Yoko.)

Mom's 'oh no second' involved flour. Instead of pastry flour, the cupboard contained only whole-wheat flour. Mom was crestfallen because the grocery stores were already closed.

"Why don't you make it with this flour?" I asked. "I'll eat it." At twelve the thought of waiting a whole other day for pie seemed an eternity. Mom was reluctant but agreed to try. A while later two magnificent pies were removed from the oven. When they cooled, the filling was perfect. Unfortunately, the crust was hard as rock.

My father muttered something about a jackhammer and headed for the garage. Jay claimed not be hungry - the first time in seventeen years - and beat a hasty retreat.

"Ray would you like some pie?" Mom asked hopefully.

It was a Hemmingway moment: a moment of truth. Would I turn tail and run or do the right thing? Then I had a sudden inspiration.

"Mom, I'd love some pie. Can I have some whipping cream on top and eat it in my room?"

Mom, elated by my enthusiasm, was only too happy to acquiesce. I slipped out the kitchen door and padded down the hall. I signaled Midnight to follow me. Safely ensconced in my room, I made short work of the whipping cream and then devoured the apple pie filling. It was delicious. Then I turned back to Midnight.

"Lucky girl! I only ate the filling but you get the whole pie!"

Midnight was willing and after much chewing managed to swallow the evidence. I opened the door and she headed straight for the water dish.

"Why on earth is the dog so thirsty?" my father asked no one in particular.

I returned my empty plate to the kitchen.

Mom was beaming. "You ate the whole piece?"

I couldn't lie but it didn't seem wrong to be diplomatic. "It's all gone and it was so good I'd like another piece after supper tomorrow!"

"Of course," Mom replied happily.

I was happy too. It's not every boy who does something so good and noble for his mother.

The next night after supper I headed down the hall, pie in hand and signaled for Midnight to come. She seemed reluctant but eventually followed me. Back in my room, I made short work of the pie filling and the whipping cream. Now it was Midnight's turn. A boy should never lie to his mother but a dog is another matter entirely.

"You eat the crust, Midnight," I ordered. "It's good for you!"

After much chewing, Midnight fled my room and hurried back to the water dish. My dad wondered aloud if the dog had diabetes.

The following evening, Mom gave me another piece of pie. As I headed down the hall, the dog jumped to its feet and bolted down the stairs.

"We have got to take this dog to the vet," my dad said letting her outside.

"Traitor!" I cursed under my breath.

I returned to my room. I ate the whipping cream and the filling but the piecrust remained. I couldn't sneak it into the garbage, someone was sure to see me. More importantly, I couldn't risk hurting Mom's feelings. So I ate the crust. And for the first time in my life I actually felt sorry for the dog.

The next evening as Mom headed for the kitchen, I piped up, "Mom, I was thinking. It's not fair for me to get all the pie. Jay and Dad should have some too!"

A look of panic crossed their faces until Mom said, "No, they had their chance. Both pies are for you, you lucky boy!"

Dad and Jay started grinning. While Mom was busy cutting me a huge hunk of apple-filled concrete, Midnight made herself scarce. As I passed the stairs, I saw her hiding out in the basement. She appeared to be laughing.

The best-laid plans often go awry. Even when the intended dupe is a dog.

These days Mom doesn't bake anymore. So whenever my sister Thea visits she makes the pies. And I always make sure she has exactly the ingredients she needs - especially the flour. After all, I don't have a dog anymore.

The Day Sandra Bullock Came to Town

"Fate loves the fearless."
~ *James Russell Lowell* ~

You can't fight fate.

Simply put, I believe there's one special person out there we're destined to be with forever. I'd almost given up hope of finding my special person until fate stepped in one Father's Day weekend a few years ago.

Jay had travelled to the Father's Day Show and Shine in Qualicum Beach, to take pictures of the classic cars. That evening he dropped by with some photos and fate began to reveal its hand.

"You'll never guess whose picture I took today!" he exclaimed excitedly.

"Whose?"

"Your favourite movie star!"

"Fred Flintstone?"

"How many times do I have to tell you Fred Flintstone is not a real person?"

"He is too."

"Never mind that. This was your favourite female movie star."

"Sandra Bullock?"

"Yup. I was taking a picture next to the café and a woman accidentally got in the shot. When I got my pictures developed it was Sandra Bullock."

"Are you sure?"

"I asked one of the car show sponsors and he said she was in town."

"You lucky dog!"

"Well here's the really interesting part. When I took her picture she gave me a quizzical look. It was almost like she'd seen me before."

Suddenly I knew that the universe had shifted and that fate was intervening in my life. I calmly explained it to Jay:

"I know exactly why she gave you that look. She thought you were me."

"What?"

"Well, we do look somewhat alike. She no doubt read my column in the paper, was overwhelmed by my sophisticated sense of humour and fell in love with my picture. She acted surprised because she thought you were me."

"Are you insane?"

"Not at all. She was just too shy to introduce herself. She probably wants me to write her next picture."

Dead silence ensued. Jay was no doubt awestruck at the very prospect of having an internationally famous brother.

"You are not going to Hollywood."

"It could happen."

"Yeah, and my cat could cough up a perfect spinach soufflé."

"Really?"

"No!"

"Still that would be neat: a cat that coughs up gourmet dinners. Hey wait a minute, you're just trying to get me off the topic."

"Desperately."

"People read my column."

"Yes, Mom does."

"Are you implying that Mom gives me pity compliments?"

"Never mind. Look Ray, Sandra Bullock is not waiting to hear from you."

"Hear from me? Now there's an idea. I'll send her some columns. Who's to say a movie star couldn't fall in love with a local columnist? After all, I'm a good speller."

"Right, but can you spell 'restraining order?' Besides, you've never even met her."

"I'll have my people call her people."

"You don't have any people!"

"I'll set up an intimate supper at the fanciest restaurant

in town. And just wait until they find out a celebrity is coming to dinner. They'll roll out the red carpet that night! Oh yeah, and I bet they'll treat Sandy pretty well too."

"Sandy?"

"All of her closest friends call her Sandy," I sniffed.

"How would you know?"

"I have my sources."

"*People* magazine is not a source. Anyway, I gotta go."

"Okay but don't be too envious when Sandy and I get married. It'll be the first time for both of us. Gee, I hope I can find my old tuxedo before the wedding."

"But she's already been married and divorced!"

"She has? But my *People* says she's never been married."

Jay picked up the magazine. "This *People* magazine is over fifteen years old. Maybe should buy a new copy once in a while."

Jay and I haven't discussed Sandra Bullock since that night. Jealousy, I suppose. Still, I've decided not to ask her out now that I know she's just been through a bad breakup. I'll give her a little time to heal. I only hope she can stand the disappointment.

As for this year's car show, there's a hot rumour that Olivia Wilde is coming to town. The latest *People* says she's single and looking for love. I'm not surprised. You can't fight fate.

Now where did I put that tuxedo?

That Sinking Feeling

"A ship in port is safe, but that's not what ships are built for."
~ Grace Murray Hopper ~

Whenever my father saw a car accident, he'd stop and direct traffic until the authorities arrived. He always wanted to be a cop. The summer I was ten he got within twelve square feet and a gallon of primer of fulfilling his dream.

Dad always wanted a speedboat too - a sporty, fast, sexy speedboat. My mother didn't see the need for speed. I, of course, was immediately on Dad's side. Imagining a career as a boat racer, I lobbied her relentlessly - to no avail.

Dad was attempting to convince her one afternoon when my brother asked, "If you get a speedboat will you take us water-skiing, Dad?"

Dad looked supremely irritated but then suddenly his visage changed. Unexpectedly he replied, "Why yes, yes I will." He turned to Mom and said, "If these boys want to learn water-skiing, I'll definitely need a speedboat!"

Mom seemed strangely mollified by this logic and I made a mental note never to play poker with my brother.

The next morning we headed to the marina. The speedboats were much too expensive. It looked hopeless until the salesman had a revelation. "I just remembered. We got a 75 horsepower police boat in yesterday. It's cheap too." At the mention of the word 'police' my Dad's eyes began to gleam. At the word 'cheap,' they positively glowed.

When Dad's new toy was delivered late that afternoon, it still had its 'Pickering Police' markings. The letters were a foot high and stretched six feet across the bow on both sides. Mom thought Dad should paint over them but he wanted to patrol the lake and watch "the malefactors straighten up" as we cruised by. Mom went inside to make supper muttering something about men and children.

After Jay and I climbed in, Dad called the dog aboard and we took off with a tremendous burst of speed. Dad was positively gleeful as boat after boat yielded him right of way. An hour later he triumphantly pulled up to the dock, jumped out and headed inside for supper.

Early the next morning the marina called. "Mr. Smit, are you aware your boat is drifting in the middle of Cook's Bay? What kind of idiot forgets to tie up a boat?"

Dad slammed down the receiver and bolted out the door with my brother, the dog and me in hot pursuit. When we got to the dock Dad stared in disbelief at the empty space where a boat should have been. Suddenly both Jay and I got the sinking feeling we were in the wrong place at the wrong time.

Dad gave Jay a baleful glare and said, "What kind of idiot forgets to tie up a boat? You got off after me. You should have tied up the boat!" He stormed back toward the cottage muttering about irresponsible teenagers.

Jay turned and glared at me with the same miserable face Dad was just wearing. "What kind of idiot forgets to tie up a boat? You got off after me. You should have tied up the boat!" Then he stomped off muttering about stupid ten-year-olds.

I looked around dejectedly until I saw the dog. I gave her a baleful glare.

"What kind of idiot forgets to tie up a boat? You got off after me. You should have tied up the boat!" I turned heel and left Midnight to consider her sins.

Jay and I decided to forgive, forget and flee. We headed for the hedges behind the cottage but Dad was already there inspecting the shrubbery. He seemed not to hear Mom calling him. The Pickering police were on the phone. Jay and I beat a hasty retreat. We were fifty yards away when Mom found Dad in the bushes. My mother is soft-spoken to a fault but I could almost swear I heard her ask, "What kind of idiot forgets to tie up a boat?"

That afternoon, after the payment of a small fine, Mom insisted that Dad paint over the 'Pickering Police' markings. Dad reluctantly agreed. But, unbeknownst to Mom, he used a temporary water-based latex primer. And that's why every spring the words 'Pickering Police' mysteriously reappeared on the bow. I think he hoped to slip out onto the lake some late April morning before Mom noticed.

She noticed.

For the rest of his days, Dad fulfilled his constabulary cravings watching endless episodes of Columbo. Forty years of dreams dashed by twelve square feet and a gallon of latex primer.

I Told You So!

*"The most insufferable people aren't the ones who think
they're right.
It's the people who actually are."*
~ *Your author* ~

I drive a 1984 Pontiac and it's beginning to show its
age – not unlike me. Maybe that's why I'm so fond of it.
Until recently it was a paragon of reliability and good
looks. But now it's just a rusting heap of bad habits.

Every morning for the past year, the old gal greeted me
with a huge plume of acrid smelling smoke. Naturally, I
did nothing. "Cars coss moe knee." So do mechanics. But
each day the plumes got bigger until even NORAD began
questioning the mushroom clouds over Parksville. It was
obvious that something needed to be done immediately –
but to reiterate, cars coss moe knee. Still, I felt sorry for
the sad-eyed asthmatic children pitifully clutching their
inhalers as I drove by.

Jay is scary smart when it comes to cars and
astrophysics. Sometimes I think he should combine his
talents and become a quantum mechanic. Despite his
expertise, I didn't want to tell him about my smoking car.
Not only would he insist that I fix it, he'd know exactly
what was wrong. And if there's anything I like less than
spending money, it's Jay being right. So I reluctantly
went to visit my mechanic for an estimate instead.

"Given the amount of smoke your trailing, I'm
guessing it's a head gasket or a cracked cylinder head.
Usually runs about eighteen hundred."

"Eighteen hundred!"

"Yes, but we don't want the job."

"But why?"

"Your car's too old. Nobody here wants to work on it."

Like most people over forty, I've faced my share of ignominy. I've been cut from the track squad, shunned by a former best friend and dumped by more women than I care to count. But this was a first. My mechanic had fired me!

Not knowing what else to do, I relented and went to my brother. He looked at the smoke and shook his head. "It's a good old car. So maybe you should change your oil once in a while. You have a valve problem."

"You're wrong," I sniffed. "The mechanic says it's a head gasket."

"Tell you what, I know a good mechanic nearby. Go see if he doesn't agree with me."

An hour later I pulled up to the repair shop. The owner came bounding up the driveway. "Thought you said it was a junker. It's a nice old Pontiac!" he declared.

I liked him right away – obviously a man of taste and refinement.

He started the car and checked the exhaust. "No smoke now," he said. "Just in the morning, I bet. It's the valves. Probably run you less than two hundred."

I suddenly liked him even more. At last someone was making sense.

"By the way, when's the last time you changed the oil?" he asked.

I mumbled something about Y2K and quickly changed the subject. The next morning I was smoke free! Yes sir, my new mechanic was absolutely right. And Jay? Well, maybe it was just a lucky guess.

A few weeks later a new problem surfaced. The Pontiac wouldn't start. My brother declared the alternator "shot."

I disagreed, "It's only a few years old."

"New starter, new battery, bad alternator," Jay insisted most insufferably.

A few days later, with rapidly dimming headlights, I stopped at a nearby garage for an opinion.

"My brother thinks it's the alternator."

The tech hooked it up to some wires. "Nope, it's producing 14.5 volts."

"He thinks it might be switching off and on."

"You're brother's not a mechanic. It needs major electrical work. Get rid of it."

The next morning I called my new mechanic. He ordered an alternator and told me to come right over. When I arrived he hooked up the voltmeter. "Hmm. 14.5 volts."

"Jay says it might be cutting in and out."

"Good point. Let's see what it does." Ten minutes later it dropped to 12 volts. "It's the alternator," he explained.

An hour later the car was running perfectly. My mechanic was right again. So was Jay but that was just an irritating coincidence.

It's like I said, the most insufferable people aren't the ones who think they're right. It's the people who actually are. Especially if he's your brother.

Happy motoring.

SHUT UP!

"Manners are the oil that lubricates society."
~ Anonymous ~

My father was a stickler for manners. "Children should be seen and not heard!" He must have told me that a million times. And my father was somebody you didn't cross if you were smart. Unfortunately, I wasn't always smart:

When I was eight, Mom and Dad had a barbecue for their friends. The back yard was packed and Dad gave me strict instructions. "You are not to address adults by their first names. You will address them as 'Sir,' or as 'Mr. Jones.' Is that clear?"

"Yes, Sir!" I replied already formulating a smart-alecky plan.

Dad took me outside and Mrs. Wilson walked over to say hello.

"Hi, Ray. Are you having a good time?"

"Yes, Sir!" I giggled, unable to resist temptation.

She looked confused and Dad gave me a warning glance. Just then Mr. Wilson wandered over.

"Hello, Ray."

"Hello, Mr. Jones."

"Our name is Wilson," whispered Mrs. Wilson patting me on the head.

"Yes Sir, Mr. Jones" I replied.

"Why doesn't he just call us Nel and Bill? It might be easier."

Dad nodded politely. Then he turned and gave me a look that could curdle cream. Needless to say, I didn't call them Nel and Bill.

By the time I was twelve my twisted sense of humour had full reign. At one of my folks' parties Mr. Stone asked me what I wanted to be when I grew up.

"A pet psychiatrist."

Dad looked pleased. A doctor, now there was a suitable calling!

"Why a 'pet' psychiatrist?"

"That way I could tell whether your Great Dane's gone insane."

Dad looked less pleased.

"We have a spaniel," Mr. Stone replied wryly.

"Well then I'd know if your cocker was off his rocker."

He said stiffly, "We also have a border collie."

"Is she happy?"

"Why do you ask?" he replied suspiciously.

"Because you wouldn't want to own a melon collie."

Dad sent me outside to play.

As I grew older I began to realize not everyone appreciated my warped sense of humour and began reining it in. Still, every now and then a quip would escape unheeded like a passing of wind. Once Mom and Dad hired a man to build an addition on their cottage. He walked up the driveway and said, "Hi, I'm the contractor."

I replied, "Don't you find it strange that when people want to make their house bigger they hire a contractor? Shouldn't they hire an expander instead?"

He looked relieved when Mom opened the door.

Today, young people routinely call adults by their first names. Some are even on a first-name basis with their parents. If I'd ever said, "Hi, Hank," to my dad, his hand would have said hello to my backside – also known as my 'brains' when he was annoyed.

Recently I was driving up a side street when the car in front of me stopped suddenly. The teenaged driver wanted to parallel park but didn't have room to get in. I tried to back up but there was a long line of cars behind me. Assuming I was trying to steal his spot, Mr. Teen rolled down his window and started hurling expletives in my direction. Then his girlfriend gave me both barrels too – proudly displaying her middle fingers repeatedly to emphasize her pithy remarks. I thought to myself, "Ah, the veritable flower of Canadian youth." Still, I wonder what it says about our society that we have a hand gesture for every kind of insult but there isn't one to say, 'I'm sorry.' Not that it would have made much difference.

Some folks blame pop culture for the growing rudeness in our society. That may be true in part. When I was a boy, radio stations featured music or pleasant conversation. Nowadays shock jocks play gangster rap and let fly their boorish sexist and racial slurs. I think maybe it's time they shut up.

Television in no better. One of the most popular shows of my childhood was *Tiny Talent Time*. No matter how skilled or unskilled a performer, everyone was greeted with the same polite applause. Nowadays performers appear on *American Idol* where they are ridiculed, mocked and scorned. The nastier and more vicious the barbs, the higher the ratings. And don't even get me started on afternoon talk shows. My father would have been appalled by their lack of decorum.

Maybe it's old-fashioned, but I still believe that "manners are the oil that lubricates society." These days, things are just a whole lot stickier.

CHAPTER NINE:

NEW ISN'T BETTER

"Everything today is new and improved.
What was it before? Old and lousy?"
~ Rob Reiner ~

Ahead of His Time?

"Give us the tools and we will finish the job."
~ Winston Churchill ~

When I was a boy, my father had Wednesdays off. Every Wednesday morning he and Mom would go shopping and while she bought groceries, Dad would peruse the latest gadgets at Sears.

On the drive home Dad would explain why he desperately needed a band saw, a rototiller or a set of genuine imitation Ginsu knives. Mom would invariably say no – much to Dad's chagrin. But when I was twelve, they worked out a modus vivendi. Mom agreed to let Dad buy any gadget he liked – as long as it cost less than twenty dollars. That way the budget would be intact and Dad would stay out of trouble. Or so she thought until one fateful Wednesday.

That morning at breakfast, Dad was in a prickly mood. Maybe it was because we were out of 2% and he had to use Carnation evaporated skim milk on his cereal. Or maybe it was because the world was "full of long-haired hippies." He turned a baleful eye toward my Beatle style locks. "You need a haircut!"

Alarmed, I began choking until evaporated skim milk ran out my nose and back in again.

My brother Jay laughed. "What do you call that, Ray? Re-in-Carnation?"

Dad ignored him. "You could use a haircut too," he said ominously.

That afternoon after school, there was a Sears bag on the dining room table. Dad pulled out a box and extricated a pair of hair clippers.

"Gee Dad," I asked hopefully, "Did you buy a dog grooming kit?"

"In a manner of speaking," he replied as he pulled out a plastic barber's apron and several combs.

He turned on the clippers and then turned to us. "Now who's first?"

"Don't you think you should try them out on the dog?" I asked hopefully. But the dog was already beating a hasty retreat downstairs. I looked over to Jay for support. It was at that moment that I first realized he had superpowers: because he had miraculously made himself invisible. I glanced out the window and saw him running down the street at warp speed.

Dad pulled out a chair. "Sit down, boy."

Mom wandered upstairs a few minutes later. "What are you doing?" she demanded.

"Just a few haircuts and this thing will pay for itself."

"Stop!"

But it was too late. The clippers were whirring and my precious Beatle haircut was already gone. Mom let out an inadvertent, "Oh no," as she surveyed the damage. Trying to be optimistic, she said, "Maybe if we comb it creatively?" With great trepidation, I looked in the mirror. There was nothing to comb. My head looked like a casaba melon with blonde spikes. My only consolation was that Sears didn't sell do-it-yourself dentistry kits.

Jay came back an hour later with a stylish and slightly shorter haircut. Dad gave him a dirty look but said nothing. He knew when he'd been out-foxed. That night Mom put her foot down. "No more home haircuts."

"Well then," Dad replied, "if you're going to waste money on barbers, I'm going to need some hedge clippers. No point paying a gardener too."

The next Wednesday Dad arrived home from Sears with his brand new hedge clippers. An hour later, the luxuriant cedar barricade that separated our house from the neighbours was as bald as my head. The neighbours were incensed. Mom apologized profusely, confiscated the hedge clippers and hid them safely out of Dad's reach next to the barber kit.

A few months later, as I mentioned in Chapter 6, Dad had a huge elm tree cut down at the cottage. One afternoon as he surveyed the stumps we hadn't been able to split by hand, he pointed out that he could cut ten cords of firewood if he only had a chainsaw. Mom didn't even argue. So the following Wednesday Dad made a trip to Sears. Unfortunately, Dad ended up buying a cheaper electric model at a different store instead of the Sears heavy-duty gas version. Shortly thereafter he discovered that an overheated electric chainsaw was no match for a gnarled old elm stump. The motor seized and the chainsaw ended up in the garage.

A few years later Dad left this life. But his story doesn't end there. Within a year of his passing, the same schoolmates who had made fun of my ridiculous haircut began shelling out big bucks for the same preposterous pompadour. Who'd have guessed that Dad created the 'punk' look?

The hedge Dad denuded eventually died, but for the first time in years we didn't have a mosquito problem. With the later arrival of West Nile Virus who'd have predicted that Dad was at the vanguard of clinical microbiology and preventative medicine?

And the old electric chainsaw? We couldn't fix it so we never did burn that firewood. Today it's common knowledge that burning wood leads to global warming. Who'd have thought back then that Dad was an environmental trailblazer? Heck, even Al Gore would be proud.

Looking back, I think Dad should have won the Nobel Prize for chemistry, peace and fashion. As Winston Churchill so perceptively said, "Give us the tools and we will finish the job."

Dad was just a little ahead of his time.

The Good Old Days

"You can't go home again."
~ Thomas Wolfe ~

Sometimes I get nostalgic for a simpler time when people were treated with respect.

When I was a little gaffer in Ontario, my Dad always bought his gas at the local Esso station. Whenever he drove in, a uniformed attendant would run out to the pumps and ask, "How are you today, Mr. Smit? Need some gas?"

And my Dad would say, " Nice to see you, Johnny. Fill her up." Then Johnny would clean the windshield and check the oil. When the tank was full, he'd run back inside and get my Dad a free glass. That was Johnny's way of thanking Dad for his patronage. My Mom and Dad were treated like that everywhere they went: the grocery store, the department store, the bakery. Everyone knew their names and regarded them as friends.

So on my last trip to central Canada, I decided to go home again - to the wonderful little town where I was raised. And if I got some of that same wonderful service Mom and Dad got back in the good old days, well, so much the better.

My first stop was Dad's favourite gas station. The old garage with its solitary hose had been replaced with a glass enclosure and six sleek new pumps. It wasn't an Esso anymore but I pulled in anyway and waited for 'Johnny' to come running out. I waited and waited and waited. After several minutes a young man came sauntering over to the car. He wasn't wearing a uniform but he did have a name on his T-shirt.

"How are you doing, Adidas?" I asked warmly.

He gave me a withering look and said, "You're blocking the pumps."

Undeterred, I replied, "Fill her up, Adidas. My name is Mr. Smit. Oh, and could you check the oil and get the windshield."

"This is a self-serve station. If you want gas get it yourself, otherwise move along Mr. Spit."

"That's Smit with an 'M.'"

"Whatever, you say Mr. Snit just get on with it."

After filling the tank, washing the windshield and checking the oil myself, I was almost afraid to ask for my complementary glass.

Adidas was not impressed. "If you want glasses, go to Wal-Mart, I've got people waiting." And with a wave of his hand, he dismissed me.

Despite my disappointing fill-up, I decided to check out the old corner store where my Mom was known and loved. Unfortunately, it was gone too. In its place stood a brand new mini mall. I walked into the convenience store ready to soak up some small town warmth and hospitality.

"Excuse me," I asked the teenaged girl behind the counter. Where can I find the hamburger buns?"

She was talking on the phone. She looked at me derisively, rolled her eyes and waved her arm in a circle around her head. I wasn't sure if I'd hit a homerun or she was asking me to dance.

So I tried again, "Hamburger buns?"

"I'm on the phone!" she intoned with great irritation.

I wandered through the store for about five minutes until I finally found the buns. I headed back to the counter where Miss Congeniality was still chatting on the phone about some girl who was a 'skank' and about some boy who has a 'hottie.' I remembered that we were out of bug spray so I asked, "Do you have any insect repellant?"

"Buzz off!"

"No we use Muskol."

"Hang on a minute. I have to talk to some clod!"

"My name is Mr. Smit not Claude."

"Just pay for your buns and leave. I'm on the phone."

My next stop was the real estate office. I'd made an appointment with a Ms. Williams to rent a cottage. I arrived promptly at three o'clock and the secretary told me to take a seat.

"Ms. Williams will be right out."

After nearly 45 minutes a realtor wandered into the lobby. "Wanna buy a condo?"

"No, I'm waiting for Ms. Williams. I want to rent a cottage."

"Renters!" he snorted in disgust and went back to his office.

At quarter to five I asked the secretary to page Ms. Williams.

"Fine," she replied with a sigh and disappeared in the back. A few minutes later she returned with coffee.

"Is that for me," I asked hopefully. It had been a long, dry wait.

"Do I look like Juan Valdez?"

"Sorry. But where's Ms. Williams?"

"She went home early. She said to come back tomorrow."

I didn't.

When I got back the coast, I was pretty disheartened. Still the everyday things need to be done and the next morning I headed out to do some shopping. I started at the local Deli where I picked up some Dutch cheese. The owner welcomed me with a smile and I spent twenty minutes swapping stories with the other customers.

Next, I stopped in at the local grocery store. Dora started processing my order with a jovial, "Hi Ray." She always has interesting anecdotes and I was sorry when the groceries were packed and it was time to leave.

On my way home I picked up some organic veggies at the health food store. The clerk and I talked about hockey and, as always, he asked me how my Mom was feeling.

As I walked out to the car, it suddenly hit me. Thomas Wolfe was right. "You can't go home again." But that's simply because home isn't about 'where' you live it's about 'how' you live. Friendship, kindness and respect are right outside your door if you only look for them.

Oh sure, I still wax nostalgic from time to time. But then I give my head a shake.

Because these are the good old days.

Confessions Of A Tech Whiz

"For a list of all the ways technology has failed to improve the quality of life,
please press three."
~ Alice Kahn ~

"I'm joining the high tech revolution!"

"You?" my brother replied appearing mystified. "You're finally getting rid of your eight track tapes?"

"Very funny. I threw them out weeks ago!"

"Uh-huh. So what are you buying?"

"A cell phone!" I replied conspiratorially. "It'll give me that high-tech, sexy up-town image with the ladies!"

"Actually, Ray, over a billion people already have cell phones."

"But they're new to Canada, right?"

"No, I've had one for ten years."

"What? Then how come you never gave me the number?"

"Say, weren't you going to visit Mom at Chrysanthemum Lodge?"

When I got to the lodge, I ran into Nan. That was fortuitous because Nan, as well as being a great nurse, is a terrific listener.

"I'm going to buy a cell phone!" I enthused.

"Excellent," she replied. "May I suggest an elder phone?"

"An elder phone?"

"Yes, it's a low tech alternative for older people who want something basic."

"I don't think Mom needs a cell phone," I whispered.

"Well, I didn't mean for your mom, I meant for you."

"Me? But I'm young and sexy."

She smiled kindly. "Okay Ray, but do you really need text messaging, ether capability and a blackberry?"

"Of course," I replied. After all, I thought, who wouldn't want a phone that writes you love notes, lulls you to sleep and makes dessert?

When I got to the phone store, the lady offered me several options:

"This one has downloadable ringer choices."

"I guess it'll have to do." I replied airily, trying to appear nonchalant.

She gave me a strange look. "Would you like me to show you how to download them?"

"No, I'm a high tech wiz, I'm sure I can handle it."

She shrugged and handed me my new cell phone."

I picked it up and said, "Beam me up, Scotty!" Laughing at my own cleverness I gushed, "Bet you've never heard that one before."

She sighed, "Only from people who speak perfect Klingon."

It was quite a compliment!

That weekend I gave everyone my new cell phone number and headed up to Courtenay. I popped into the washroom at Tim Hortons and was standing – well, where you stand - when my cell phone suddenly went off. I'd never heard it ring before.

"Deedlie, deedlie, dee, dee, dee!"

Unfortunately, it sounded like Tinkerbell sprinkling fairy dust on Peter Pan.

"Deedlie, deedlie, dee, dee, dee!"

The last thing I wanted, while standing at the convenience, was a musical accompaniment reserved for pixies in leotards. Crashing cymbals? The sound of trumpets? Maybe some thunder? Sure! But certainly not, "Deedlie, deedlie, dee, dee, dee!"

The man at the next convenience gave me a strange look. And you can imagine what his kid had to say.

"Daddy that man tinkles when he tinkles!"

"Daddy, do you tinkle when…?"

"No! Absolutely not! Never!"

The phone kept ringing. "Deedlie, deedlie, dee, dee, dee!" Unfortunately, I had it zipped inside my jacket pocket. There was no way to get at it. So to say the least I was greatly relieved - when I was greatly relieved. I quickly washed my hands, unzipped my jacket and grabbed the phone.

"Deedlie, deedlie, dee, dee, dee!"

"Hello? Oh, hi Mom."

That brought more than a few snickers…

"Yes, Mom. Sure I can get you some biscuits. Yes, I love you too, Mom. Goodbye."

I slunk out of the bathroom and headed for the car, the sound of laughter echoing behind me.

That night, unable to sleep as I thought about my humiliation, I made a decision. A macho guy like me doesn't turn tail and run. No sir! I was going back to that donut shop. I was going back into that men's room and I was going in macho! Maybe I'd wear my cowboy hat. I didn't live in Alberta all those years for nothing! Yup, that was the answer – dress up like a range roving, tobacco spitting, nail-chewing cowboy and show those city slickers what macho was all about.

I finally fell nodded off...When I walked back into the men's room I noticed a construction worker washing his hands. The cop next to me nodded. Then an Indian Chief walked in. I looked at my cowboy hat in the mirror. What was wrong with this picture? Suddenly all of their cell phones began ringing. And they were all playing the same tune. "Macho, Macho Man, I've got to be a Macho Man."

I woke up in a cold sweat. I decided to forget about donuts for a while – although I did have the strangest urge to hear a Village People album. If only I hadn't thrown out my eight tracks!

I guess my new high-tech gadget isn't that cool after all. I sure haven't impressed any women with it. Nor have I figured out how to change the ring tone. You never know if someone important is trying to reach you so I always leave it on wherever I go. With one exception. But I think you can guess where that is.

"Deedlie, deedlie, dee, dee, dee!"

Sorry, Wrong Number

*"I don't answer the phone. I get the feeling whenever I do
that there will be someone on the other end."*
~ Fred Couples ~

As you may have guessed by now, I abhor telephones.
They are devious devices, which have blighted
humankind since their invention. Don't believe me?
Consider again Alexander Graham Bell, creator of the
cursed contrivance. Every schoolchild can relate the story
of the invention of the telephone on March 7th, 1876.
They'll tell you that Bell spilled some acid on his clothes
and called to his assistant saying, "Mr. Watson. Come
here, I need you." And we all know that Mr. Watson came
running.

Did you ever stop to ask yourself why Bell spilled acid
all over himself? It's because he wasn't paying attention
to his work. He was too busy yakking on the phone!
Which just proves my point, the phone is an evil
doohickey sent to confuse and confound us.

"But surely, you didn't always feel this way, Ray?"

You might inquire.

No, I must admit I didn't. I used to think of the phone
as a benevolent invention. That is until the first time I
used it to ask a girl for a date:

Yes, as you've probably already guessed, it was Jane. I
got her number from a friend and prepared to ask her out.
Until the very second I picked up the phone, I considered
myself the epitome of rakish charm. As I dialed, I began

to sweat. What should I say? What if she turned me down?

Unfortunately, her mother answered.

"Hello."

"Uh, hello. Uh…is Jane there…uh…err…still?"

Her mom had a great time with that one.

"Yes, Jane is still living at home. Why do you ask? Is she planning on moving out? She's only 16 but maybe I'd better check. Jane, honey, some boy on the phone wants to know if you're planning on moving. Would you like to keep your room or shall I rent it out?"

I could barely hear her over the raucous laughter in the background. With one short telephone call my self-image was reduced from 'charming, debonair sophisticate' to 'blubbering idiot.'

But then what has the phone ever brought anyone but aggravation? Up until 1876, you could relax in the bathtub without being disturbed. But I just bet when the first two subscribers were hooked up something like this happened:

"Hello, I'm calling on behalf of Boston Carpet Cleaning with a special introductory offer. By the way, is this Mr. Alexander Graham Bell?"

"I think you may have the wrong number."

"I don't think so Mr. Bell. After all there are only two phones in the world."

Served him right!

And speaking of bathtubs, they say that the modern bathtub originated in Greece at least 500 years before the birth of Christ. Imagine being able to relax in a tub for 2400 years and never hearing a phone ring. Of course, after 2400 years in the tub you'd leave a different type of 'ring,' but personal hygiene questions are best left to doctors and punk bands.

Nevertheless, all of these irritations pale in comparison to the aggravation caused by wrong numbers. When my mom last moved she was given a new phone number. Unfortunately, it had previously belonged to 'Jed's Plumbing.' She got hundreds of calls for old Jed who I suppose had retired and gone fishing. Once, during a visit, I got so fed up with the constant interruptions that I decided to have a little fun at Jed's expense:

"Is this Jed's plumbing?"

"Nope. Jed's business has gone down the toilet."

"Jed's plumbing?"

"Nope. Jed quit. He found the plumbing business was far too draining."

I could go on….

As a columnist I'm always facing deadlines. And truth be known, I don't always feel like writing something for the paper. Sometimes I'd rather take a walk or play tennis. One time I even thought up a bunch of excuses so my editor would give me a week off. Only problem was that I had to phone him:

"Uh…hello. Is the editor there…uh…err…still?"

"Well let me check. Hey, boss, are you *still* here or will you be editing the New York Times today. Some 'blubbering idiot' on line two wants to know. Never mind, he just hung up."

I hate the telephone.

Folklore Ain't What It Used To Be

"Sign , sign , everywhere a sign."
~ Five Man Electrical Band ~

Folklore ain't what it used to be.

In the good old days, country folk watched everyday events and looked for their symbolic value as portents, omens or signs. A seemingly ordinary occurrence could hold great importance for our forefathers. I hearken back to those golden days when an eclipse foretold momentous political changes and a songbird lighting on your picket fence was a sure sign of good fortune.

I was thinking of that yesterday when a hornet (the insect not the car) landed on my patio. The hornet had somehow landed on his back and as it struggled to right itself. I had an inspiration. Perhaps the hornet's struggle was a symbol, just like the ones used in folklore, low those many years ago.

Perhaps its struggle was a lesson in the value of hard work and perseverance just like the folklore of the past.

I began to mentally compose the grand story of the diligent little hornet that never quits despite formidable odds. It would be an inspirational story of a brave little creature that overcomes adversity and eventually flies away victorious.

In my mind's eye I could see people reading my story and nodding their heads gravely as they shared in the valuable lesson. Perhaps a national newspaper chain would syndicate it throughout Canada; maybe even the whole world.

Perhaps the Prime Minister would speak of it in the House of Commons. Heck maybe the President would discuss it with small children as they visited the Oval Office.

I wondered if I might even become a celebrity and be invited on *Canada AM*? Oh, how I wish Valerie Pringle hadn't left the show. She was so cute.

"Yes, I'm glad you enjoyed my story, Valerie. And may I say how much my family enjoys your fine potato chips."

Maybe I'd even get a special interview with Oprah. Who knows, maybe we'd get to be friends and she'd call me Ray and I'd call her Miss Winfrey. Well, as they say, "go big or go home." Maybe I'd even be on CNN:

"Hello and welcome to Piers Morgan Live. Tonight's guests are actress Rosanna Arquette and inspirational author of the Hornet Story, Ray Smit.

"Why, hello Miss Arquette, I'm so glad you loved my story. Why no, I'm not doing anything after the show. Yes, as a matter of fact, I am single. A late supper? Well, I'm doing Letterman tomorrow but I think I can make the time.

As I happily daydreamed about the future, my eye turned back to the hornet. It was struggling furiously.

"What tremendous willpower this little creature has, I thought as I scribbled down my observations. What a marvelous story this was going to be. Perhaps it might make a good novel or even a motion a picture.

"And now presenting the Academy Award for Best Original Screenplay is Sandra Bullock. And the nominees are Steven Spielberg, Ron Howard, Ang Lee, Peter

Jackson and Ray Smit for the Hornet Story. Receiving the Academy Award for best original screenplay is… Ray Smit for the Hornet Story."

" Why thank you Miss Bullock. No, I'm not doing anything after the show. A late supper with you and Kim Basinger? Okay, as long as no one invites Jay Leno along. He's been begging me to do the Tonight Show for months and I just don't have the time."

I turned back to the hornet. It had stopped moving. Catching its breath, I surmised. A few minutes passed.

"Hmmm. Gathering it's strength for one last effort, I thought. "That'll make it an even better story.

A few more minutes passed. The hornet was slowly beginning to shrivel up in the sun.

Like, I said, folklore ain't what it used to be.

CHAPTER TEN:

WHAT EVERY MAN SHOULD KNOW

"Macho does not prove mucho."
~ Zsa Zsa Gabor ~

MY MACHISMO GETS 20 MILES PER GALLON

"Everyone rises to their level of
incompetence."
~ Laurence J. Peter ~

It's embarrassing to admit it, but I know nothing about cars. That may not a big deal for some people, but it's really disconcerting when your brother is a great backyard mechanic. On weekends, his house is full of 'car guys' and the debates rage for hours about torque converters, superchargers and tunnel rams.

Machismo, on the weekend, is defined by our in-depth knowledge of every RPM, gapped plug and fuel injector. Regrettably I have no mechanical aptitude, which leaves me little ammunition for defending my precious male ego. I try to be one of the guys but our conversations often end up like this recent one:

Jack started the festivities with a remark about his split-window:

"Why don't you take it up to the auto glass place?" I asked. "They've got a sale on windshields this week."

"No," my brother replied with a sigh. "A split-window is the nick-name for a 1963 roadster."

"Well," I said trying to regain my equilibrium, "I don't know much about foreign cars. I'm more of an American car fancier."

"A split-window is an American car," replied my brother irritably. "It's made in St. Louis, Missouri."

At this point, I was hearing snickers all around and made a last ditch effort to save my male pride. "I'm not a Ford or Chrysler man. I'm into Chevrolets."

"A 1963 split-window is a Chevrolet," retorted a very annoyed 300-pound expert in 20-pound cowboy boots.

"Oh," I replied cleverly deciding not to push the matter any further. After all, he had an anchor tattooed on his arm and I was beginning to get seasick. I figured the best thing to do was to bide my time until someone brought up an easier topic. A few hours later I got my chance.

"I figure a guy could pick up some extra cash by doing some port and polishing." my brother said.

I jumped in without missing a beat. "I had an old Buick once and I polished the ports on the hood all the time with chrome polish. I could give you guys some tips on which brand to buy if you like."

"Porting and polishing," replied my brother with a patronizing smile, "is a way of improving engine efficiency by grinding the cylinder head ports."

"Oh," I said trying to look nonchalant.

"Look, Ray. Why don't you just go make us all some coffee, huh?"

I could hear the muffled laughter coming from the living room while the coffee was brewing. And for some strange reason, the anchor guy started questioning my dancing ability. Because I clearly heard him ask my brother if I was a little light on my feet.

Well, I told you that I don't know anything about cars. But this weekend is going to be different. My brother's invited some friends over to talk hockey. I just know that the Bruins won't stand a chance against the Yankees or the Lakers in the Super Bowl. Those guys are going to be so impressed!

How I Lost The Battle of the Sexes

*"Nobody will ever win the battle of the sexes.
There's too much fraternizing with the enemy."*
~ Henry Kissinger ~

I started fraternizing with the enemy at an early age. I don't mean to brag but by the time I was four, I already had a girlfriend. Feminism wasn't an issue for me then. I was four, she was three and we were in love. I thought that was normal. Shortly thereafter my folks put the house for sale and moved away.

When I was nine I had another girlfriend. It was love! She was the cutest girl in grade 4. Shortly before grade 5 my folks put the house for sale and moved again. Then, just before high school, I met another cute girl. This time my parents sat me down for 'the talk.' Realtors cost money.

Mom and Dad were 'old school.' They taught me to treat girls with respect: "Make sure to open the door for a lady and be a gentleman at all times." And that's what I've always tried to do. At thirteen I thought I had the world by the tail. There was only one fly in the ointment: women's liberation.

Now don't get me wrong. Even as a teenager I believed in economic equality, equal pay and all that. But there was no way I was going to make the beds. That was women's work!

I remember my first day at high school. Some girls were walking down the hallway and I held the door for them.

"Male chauvinist!" one of them snorted as she walked by. "I suppose you think women are incapable of opening doors."

"Yes, err...I mean no. Oh boy."

"Creep!"

Welcome to the real world.

A few days later, faced with a similar dilemma, I let the door close behind me.

"Don't you know enough to open a door for a lady?" the girl behind me snorted.

"Yeah, creep!" added her friend.

Feminism was confusing to me. As I got older I learned not to 'step in it' quite as often, but I was still hopelessly old-fashioned. When I was seventeen, I met the love of my life. Yes, Jane! She was a feminist and one of the most adept people I've ever known. As I mentioned earlier, my male chauvinist instincts kicked in. I wasn't about to lose to a girl! So we competed at everything: bowling, grades, swimming, summer jobs. You name it. And Jane won at bowling, grades, swimming, and summer jobs. You name it!

Jane was no fool. Eventually she moved on. Single again, I slunk off to university. That's where I met Kate. Kate was one of the most beautiful women I'd ever seen. And she never talked about feminist issues! Yes sir, I was home free. That is until she asked me if she shouldn't stop the "thoroughly anachronistic" habit of shaving her legs. After the first wave of panic passed, I muttered something about Nair and pleaded the fifth. She dumped me soon afterward. I don't blame her.

For thirty years men fought the feminist revolution tooth and nail.

"No way my wife is working! No way my wife is driving! No way my wife is cleaning the gutters… Hey wait a minute!"

That enormous hollow noise you heard nearly two decades ago was the sound of three billion Homer Simpsons slapping their foreheads in unison and saying, "D'oh!" It was July 29th, 1995: the day that men achieved self-awareness. Truthfully, we're not sure of the exact date. There wasn't a woman there to tell us to write it down.

Still nothing ever remains the same. I've recently encountered several eligible women who've wistfully whispered, "I'm not a feminist, you know."

And I invariably reply, "I'm sorry, but I'm too emancipated to go back to oppressing women."

As for Henry Kissinger's famous quotation about nobody ever winning the battle of the sexes, I think Henry was a hopeless optimist. It was game set and match long before Bobby Riggs got his clock cleaned by Billy Jean King.

Still, I've decided to be graceful in defeat.

So, if you're looking for an old-fashioned hard-working guy who's ready to take on responsibility, it's too late. I'll be watching Oprah. And if I ever marry, my wife can be the breadwinner.

After all, she told me to make the bed. Now she can lie in it.

Cool Hand Ray

"I am not an adventurer by choice but by fate."
~ Vincent Van Gogh ~

When I was a kid, I wanted to be macho. I wanted to sneer at misfortune, smirk at adversity and smile at danger. I longed to be as cool as Richard Burton in *Where Eagles Dare.* Unfortunately, I've never had his kind of unflappable charm.

On the other hand, my brother is naturally cool. Always was. For instance, when he was a teen, his friends used to drop by for advice. And Jay would tell them how to tune up their cars or build things. Girls would come over too. Lots of girls! They'd arrive with homemade cookies or cakes, nonchalantly asking if Jay was around. And if I helped myself to one of those treats they'd give me a look that could crack a mirror at fifty paces.

"Those are for Jay!" they'd hiss.

I bet they wouldn't have talked that way to Richard Burton!

Once on a Grade 5 school trip, someone from our class got lost in downtown Toronto. And he cried and cried like a little girl. Fortunately, he found the school bus by sheer accident and no one else ever knew a thing about it. I bet my brother wouldn't have cried. Even in the most embarrassing situations, he's imperturbable.

For example, his doctor recently told him that he needed a prostate exam. Now most men (and all extra-terrestrials) will tell you there's no way to be cool during a rectal probe. Au contraire. The doctor had just started the procedure when Jay asked him if he wouldn't mind using two fingers instead of the customary one.

"Why on earth would you want me to do that?"

"Because I'd like to get my second opinion right away."

Now that's cool! And, of course his doctor roared. Although, I do question the wisdom of making anyone laugh while his finger is up your you know what. But that's just me. I'm not cool.

Speaking of embarrassment, someone once told me a story about a middle-aged man who went to an elderly physician for a prostate checkup. The doctor made him get up on the examining table on all fours with trousers in full retreat. Then the old fellow headed down the hallway in search of some exam gloves. Unfortunately, he forgot to close the door behind him. Just then a woman walked by accompanied by a nurse. The man, acutely embarrassed, tried unsuccessfully to reach for a nearby lab coat with his right index finger.

The woman exclaimed "Oh dear! What is that?"

"It looks like a short-haired pointer," the nurse retorted.

"Ugly breed," the woman responded.

"Indoubetedly," replied the nurse.

I can only hope the story is apocryphal.

Luckily for me, my doctor is a civilized fellow. He's not only a brilliant clinician but knows Monty Python by heart. In other words, he's cooler than any doctor has a right to be. Recently during an examination, he found a protuberance on my-err-posterior protruding part. Unfortunately, it had to be removed. I tried to think of something funny to say. It seemed preferable to crying. When the whole ugly procedure was completed all I could offer was, "I don't know how to say thank you."

The good doctor nonchalantly replied, "I don't believe they have a greeting card for something like this just yet." I only wish I could be that cool.

Recently, I heard a story about my hero Richard Burton. During a stage performance, he was wearing armor. Halfway through the play he felt the overwhelming call of nature. Unfortunately, there was no way to remove his suit of mail without stopping the show. So he continued. Unfortunately, during a dramatic turn, nature took its inevitable course. To his credit Burton finished the show without missing a line. Although some of the other actors did think he was perspiring a great deal. Now that's cool – in a manner of speaking.

As I've gotten older, I've had to face many unpleasant truths. One is that I'll never be as cool as my brother Jay or my doctor or Richard Burton. Still, in the long run, perhaps it doesn't matter. At least I've never wet my pants in front of an audience or cried like a little girl in downtown Toronto.

Not that you know of anyway.

Real Men Do It In The Woods

"I hate the outdoors. To me the outdoors is where the car is."
~ Michael Moncur ~

Like all guys, I like to think of myself as a real man. Growing up my heroes were Roy Rogers and Davey Crockett. You can't get more real than that. Those guys practically oozed testosterone; virile men who could survive outdoors with nothing but a pocketknife and a coonskin cap.

I was raised in Toronto, which made it difficult to be a cowboy or a frontiersman. The closest thing we had to the prairie was the empty lot down the street; the nearest thing to a forest was a thirty-inch shrub on our front lawn. Despite my city environment, I was confident that I could live off the land just like my TV heroes. That is, if Mom would ever let me have a pocketknife.

Reality and self-image are seldom congruent. I began to find that out when I was ten. Mom and Dad bought a tent, which we set it up in the back yard. I begged the folks for a campout. Despite Mom's worries, Dad agreed. Yes sir, Buckaroo Ray was gonna do some livin' off the land. With my cowboy hat tilted rakishly, my faithful dog at my side and my trusty pocketknife for protection; I'd be a young Joe Cartwright. I could imagine myself cooking over an open fire while bravely protecting the Ponderosa from rustlers and horse thieves.

That night, I invited my buddy David to a campout. Unfortunately, I didn't have a cowboy hat, Dad nixed the campfire and Mom was unyielding about the pocketknife. Never mind! There was still my trusty dog, Midnight. At nine o'clock David and I headed outside and I whistled for my faithful canine companion. She got up stiffly, ignored the open door and climbed onto our old couch. Then she promptly fell asleep. Undeterred, David and I headed outside to tell ghost stories and live like cowboys. It was a dark night - spooky and cold.

 Strangely we didn't feel like telling ghost stories. We unrolled our sleeping bags at 9:10 and ate some marshmallows at 9:15. The back gate started creaking at 9:20 - was it the wind or an axe wielding mutant from the planet Zylon? We ran inside for dear life.

Dad looked at his watch and nodded to my mother. "Twenty minutes! Right on schedule. Told you not to worry."

My next outdoor adventure came in my teens when a bunch of us went camping at Lake Simcoe. My best friend Brad and I shared a tent and our respective girlfriends shared another. Despite my nasty sore throat, the evening was wonderfully romantic. As I settled in for the night, however, I realized that my threadbare old sleeping bag was no match for the cold. I was awake shivering most of the night. At about three AM I noticed a great big nose protruding into our tent. I maintain it was a grizzly, but some say it was my rubber boot. I would have attacked it I only had a pocketknife. I yelled to Brad,

"Wake up, it's a bear!" Unfortunately, given my terror and my sore throat, I sounded remarkably like a girl screaming for Justin Bieber. Brad told me to shut up and went back to sleep.

The next morning, mortified, I hoped that no one had heard my outburst. Brad, always a true friend, said nothing. And my girlfriend, Jane? She just smiled and asked if I'd like to borrow her Lady Schick.

So, truth be known, I'm not an outdoorsman. My idea of roughing it is staying at a three-star resort. I'm the kind of guy Roy Rogers would have dismissed as a 'tenderfoot.' But now that I'm flirting with fifty, I'm not going to let that worry me. No sir! Because deep down, I know I could be an outdoorsman if I wanted to.

Well, at least if Mom ever lets me have that pocketknife.

Words To Remember

"Greater love hath no man than this, that a man lay down his life for his friends."
~ John 15:13 ~

Jan Rutgers entered the train station in North Holland hoping to look inconspicuous. He was carrying a large suitcase. He'd done this a dozen times before. So far his luck had held. It needed to. It was 1943 and many Jewish families hidden in southern Holland were counting on him – though most had never met him or even knew he existed.

As he approached the train, he stopped suddenly and drew in a sharp breath. Nazi guards! They were checking everyone. As nonchalantly as possible he changed direction and headed to the men's room. He stayed a few moments leaving the suitcase behind. He cursed his luck, because the suitcase contained more than thirty pounds of fresh meat obtained from an underground contact. If he'd been caught, he'd have faced certain arrest.

My Uncle Jan's exploits were a source of pride for our family. In the daytime he was the nondescript office manager of a dental practice. But at night he worked for the underground; hiding members of the Resistance and their families.

My father and most of my uncles were also members of the Resistance. My mother recalls many evenings when my father would slip out after curfew. The next morning word would spread that a bridge had been blown up or an airfield attacked. My father offered no explanations. My mother asked for none. In our family only my Uncle Johan seemed uninterested in the war effort.

Loose lips sink ships. Unfortunately, someone tipped off the local Nazi command about Uncle Jan's activities. They came for him one winter night. Luckily he wasn't home. He often spent his evenings at the local station collecting stray pieces of coal from passing trains rumbling through on their way to Germany. Although it was officially verboten, he gathered enough coal each week to heat an elderly friend's house. He also brought her food. She spoke of him often after the war – always referring to him as her 'son.'

Uncle Jan went into hiding but continued working for the Resistance. One afternoon carrying forged identity papers he was stopped by a Nazi patrol. They conducted a routine search and found dozens of counterfeit food ration coupons in his jacket. He was arrested and his true identity quickly discovered. In 1944, he was sent to a concentration camp.

Given a job in the kitchen, he used every opportunity to smuggle food out to sick prisoners. He was eventually caught. The punishment? He was assigned to the laundry detail. Then, after working long shifts in the sweltering heat, he was forced to stand at attention - outside in subzero temperatures. Several days later he died. The official cause of death was meningitis.

Uncle Jan did not act alone. His underground meat suppliers were my Aunt Win and Uncle Hendrik. They hid several Jewish children in their home during the war. My Uncle Hendrik would send them outside to play even when Nazi patrols were near. It was brilliant reverse psychology. The Nazis never suspected that children playing in the front yard were Jewish.

And the counterfeit food ration coupons and fake identity papers? They were almost certainly created using the printing presses hidden in my Uncle Johan's basement. Despite criticism for his lack of 'patriotism,' he kept his leadership role in the Resistance a closely held secret until the war ended.

The happiest moment in Dutch history was likely May 5, 1945. That was the day Canadian soldiers liberated Holland. They came from B.C. mill towns, Alberta farms, central Canadian cities and Maritime fishing villages. All risked their lives so that families like mine could be free. They jeopardized their hopes, their dreams; their very futures for the sake of others. Some were buried in Holland. Some returned home injured in body or in spirit. But all contributed to the great post-war democracy we take for granted.

There are no words to adequately thank them for their

sacrifice. And although they say little about the war, their heroism speaks volumes.

Our family's experiences in WWII were not uncommon. Many families – most families - have great grandparents who served with distinction. We can only thank them but, if we're truly grateful, we should do one thing more. Let every family chronicle the tales of service our grandparents and great grandparents are willing to share. The cost of freedom is high. Their stories should not be lost.

'Greater love hath no man than this, that a man lay down his life for his friends.'

Something every person should remember.

Lest we forget.

CHAPTER ELEVEN:

HOLIDAYS AND HOLY DAYS

"My candle burns at both ends;
It will not last the night;
But, ah my foes, and, oh, my friends –
It gives a lovely light."
~ Edna St. Vincent Millay ~

You Say You Want A Resolution?

[I] have known the evenings, mornings, afternoons,
I have measured out my life with coffee spoons;

~T.S. Eliot ~

When I was ten my New Year's resolution was to stay up until midnight and ring in a new year for the first time. My parents had already accepted a New Year's invitation from the neighbours but after much cajoling they agreed to cancel their plans. I was so excited I didn't sleep the night before. By nine on New Year's Eve I was fading fast. At five past eleven the phone rang and woke me up. It was Mr.Tyson from next-door asking Mom and Dad to reconsider his invitation.

Dad gave Mom a quizzical look and Mom nodded.

"Kids, we're popping over to the neighbours for a few minutes."

"But you promised," I whimpered annoyingly.

"We'll be back before you know it."

Within five minutes my fifteen year-old brother was reading his Hot Rod magazine and I was sound asleep. The next morning I woke up to sounds in the kitchen.

"Hey, I missed New Year's Eve. You fibbed!" I whined accusingly at Mom and Dad.

"No they didn't," Jay replied. "They said they'd be back before you knew it. When they came in at three-thirty you were asleep, so technically they were home before you knew it."

His logic was impeccable. Still I felt cheated. "They promised," I muttered to no one in particular.

As I was pondering my fate, I had a sudden revelation. Maybe, the folks hadn't fibbed. Maybe they were just having so much fun that they forgot all about their promise. Until then, I pretty much thought Mom and Dad's world revolved around me. It clearly didn't. And it was at that moment that the Ray-centered universe disappeared and was replaced by the one known as reality.

The next year, Mom and Dad hosted the neighbourhood New Year's party at our house. My resolution was not only to stay awake but to ensure no one forgot me again. So I formulated a plan. As the clock struck twelve the celebrations started. When the commotion died down, I crossed my legs together, furrowed my brow and let out a loud groan.

The room instantly became quiet

"What's wrong?" asked a worried Mrs. Tyson.

"Nothing. It's just that I haven't been to the bathroom - SINCE LAST YEAR!"

The house exploded with laughter. It was the first time I'd ever written a joke or made a group of adults laugh. Their reaction was a revelation and I immediately knew what I wanted to do with the rest of my life.

When I was a painfully skinny nineteen year-old, I had a falling out with my best friend. Rather than stew about it, I resolved to toughen up emotionally. Early on New Year's Eve there was a knock on the door. It was my erstwhile buddy.

"Hey Ray have you been doing some modeling?"

"No. Why?" I replied suspiciously.

"Because, I thought I saw your face on the iodine bottle."

It took all my willpower not to laugh. He offered to shake hands and let "bygones be bygones."

Too intent on nursing my grudge, I refused. It effectively ended our friendship. I soon realized that getting tough gets you nowhere and a grudge is just a roadblock on the way to happiness.

New Year's Eve 2003 was a particularly difficult one. Mom was ill and her husband Henry was in heart failure. Instead of a resolution, I offered up a New Year's prayer – I asked for one last trip to the ocean with Henry before he slipped into eternity. The answer was no. I had no choice but to accept the inevitable. And I realized that even though prayer does change things it more often changes us.

This year I made the usual resolutions: to lose weight and exercise more. But then I had another revelation. All of my resolutions were solely for my benefit. They were, at their heart, selfish.

So this year beside the usual healthy living promises, I've resolved something more: to spend more time volunteering, to visit the lonely and shut-ins and to give more generously to worthy charities like the Salvation Army and the local gospel mission.

Some lives are "measured out in coffee spoons." Mine has been measured out in New Year's eves. However you gauge your life's complications, may all your promised resolutions become your treasured revelations.

Confessions of a Halloweenie

*"All may be fair in love and war but there is none so mercenary
as a child at Halloween."*
~ Your author ~

I went trick or treating alone for the first time when I was eight.

I fully expected Mom to make me an authentic Superman costume including a cape. I drew the line at Superman's tights. Even at eight, I recognized that real men shouldn't prance around in tights – superhero or not.

Mom didn't have time to make a costume but she did buy me a cat mask. It was all they had left at Sears. Undeterred, I imagined myself stealthily darting from house to house with feline agility as I acquired mountains of chocolate bars.

I hit the streets at 5:30 only to find them replete with children lugging heavy bags of candy dreams. I felt a quick flash of panic. I'd better get moving. I headed straight for Mrs. Tyler's house. Mrs. Tyler was renowned for her delicious candy apples. A tall skeleton stopped me in my tracks. It was Wesley, a teenager from up the street.

"Where you going, Ray?"

"Mrs. Tyler's house!"

"Don't wanna go there. She didn't make candy apples this year."

He leaned over conspiratorially, "Let me give you a tip. Go to Mrs. Brady's."

"Why?"

"She's got chocolate bars!"

"Really?"

"Oh yeah, great big ones and potato chips too. You better hurry!"

"Wow, thanks, Wesley!"

I ran all the way to Mrs. Brady's house. She answered the door wearing a tattered housecoat and curlers. She bore a remarkable resemblance to Mrs. Kravitz on *Bewitched*.

She gave me a baleful glare. "What are you supposed to be?"

"A cat."

"Pretty lousy cat. Where's your tail and whiskers?"

"I dunno."

"Well, I think a lousy cat oughta sing for his supper. So sing something."

So I sang O Canada and opened my pillowcase.

"Not so fast," she directed. "Sing *God Save the Queen*."

So I sang *God Save the Queen*. Not satisfied she had me perform several pop classics and the entire score to *The Sound of Music* (I may be exaggerating slightly).

When I opened my pillowcase, she picked up a plate of Chiclets. Not chocolate bars, not potato chips…just Chiclets. I hate Chiclets! She opened a box, took out a single piece, and dropped it in my pillowcase.

"What do you say, little boy?"

Several things came to mind. But I settled for a mumbled thank you and hurried back to Mrs. Tyler's house. It was already 5:45! Skeletor was leaning against the fence.

"Have fun at Mrs. Brady's?" he snickered showing me his bag full of candy apples. I ignored him and ran up the steps.

Mrs. Tyler opened the door and exclaimed, "Ray. Where's your costume?"

My cat mask was no longer attached to my head so I was essentially running around in my street clothes.

"Why didn't you come earlier? I'm all out of candy apples. Must have had ten kids tonight dressed as skeletons. They cleaned me out. All I've got left is Chiclets."

Dejectedly, I headed to the next house. A nice man opened the door and said, "Smile for me." He was holding out a plate of chocolate bars! Smile? Just try and stop me!

"Oh my!" he said withdrawing the chocolates. "I'm a dentist and by the looks of your baby teeth, I think we better give you some sugar free gum."

Seeing my disappointment he said, "Well okay, we'll settle for some Chiclets."

When I got home at 7:30, the inside of my pillowcase was as white as the outside. Not a solitary chocolate bar or candy apple graced its interior. It was well nigh traumatic!

To this day, I can't watch, *It's The Great Pumpkin, Charlie Brown*, without sobbing uncontrollably. And I still don't trust skeletons -which is the only reason I'm not dating a supermodel. And don't even get me started on Rogers and Hammerstein. Although, I do sing *I Am Sixteen Going on Seventeen* with a certain ironic panache.

This year, I'll be popping into the grocery store on Halloween and buying as many blessed chocolate bars as I want. And, should I lose a tooth, I won't care. I'll just replace it with something white and shiny. I still have plenty of Chiclets left.

A Mother's Day Is As Good As A Rest

"My mother protected me from the world and my father threatened me with it."

~ Quentin Crisp ~

Mother's Day was revered at our house. Dad would wake my brother and me early so we could make our mother breakfast. "Your mother works hard all year. The least you can do is make her breakfast on Mother's Day. She needs her rest!"

Mom would 'ooh' and 'ah' about how wonderful the burnt eggs tasted and then Dad would send us to the kitchen to do the dishes.

"You boys clean up. Your mother needs her rest."

Of course, the mess was far more than a ten or five-year old could handle so Mom would send us outside while she cleaned up the chaos and drank a bottle of Pepto Bismol.

After breakfast, we gave Mom her presents: a lawn chair from Dad and cheap perfume from her boys. Every year she got lawn chairs and perfume, but she always acted surprised and delighted. She'd spritz on some perfume, the dog would sneeze repeatedly and then she'd clean up the wrapping paper and cards. Shortly thereafter, Dad would announce that a trip to the cottage was in order.

"Help your mother get everything ready. She needs her rest."

So Mom would make a potato salad, pack the picnic cooler and do a quick vacuum. Jay and I would be in charge of carrying things to the car. Then we'd head up to the cottage so Dad could go fishing and Mom could rest.

After fishing, Dad would hand us the catch.

"You don't expect your Mother to clean fish on Mother's Day, do you? She needs her rest!"

Mom would smile beatifically until Dad went back outside to sit in Mom's new lawn chair. Then she'd take the fish and gut them herself.

After supper, Dad would declare us ready to drive home.

"Help your mother clean up the cottage. She needs her rest!"

Then Mom would mutter something like, "Wait until Father's Day."

Mom usually fell asleep on the drive home. I think it was probably because she was so relaxed from getting our help all day. She always said that any Mother's Day was a happy one as long as her family was with her. And Dad didn't seem to mind the extra work.

Three years after my father passed, she married Henry, another inveterate outdoorsman. In 1983, they decided to take a camping trip to Ontario. Mom wanted a comfortable motorhome but Henry decided to renovate their van instead. He built a homemade bed, jerry-rigged a Coleman stove and installed a porta-potti. Mom wanted 'running' water but Henry bought a four-liter jug of spring water as an alternative putting it between the front seats. Unfortunately, every time they went up a hill it would slide to the back of the van and Mom had to go 'running' after it.

They hit the open road just before Mother's Day and stopped at Revelstoke. The following morning Henry was hungry and grandly offered to make breakfast. He brewed some coffee and prepared camping-style toast and fried eggs in their iron skillet. Then he heated up the best part of any Dutch breakfast: a foot-long sausage. Just then a seagull swooped down, landed on the eggs and toast, grabbed the sausage and flew away. After a long silence Mom said, "Henry, I think your breakfast is for the birds!" and set about preparing a new one from scratch.

They got to Manitoba on Mother's Day where Henry grandly offered to make breakfast again. "You need your rest."

Mom declined the offer. She was busy fixing breakfast when a black bear suddenly appeared. She and

Henry retreated to the van. Surprisingly, the bear ignored Mom's cooking, preferring the delights of a nearby garbage can. There was a good joke in there somewhere, but Henry – evaluating Mom's perturbed visage - was wise enough not to tell it - especially on Mother's Day.

As always, this Mother's Day my brother and I will be visiting our Mom. We won't ask her to go camping, cook breakfast, do dishes or even gut fish. That is unless she really wants to! In which case, why not? After all, she needs her rest.

Love's Labour Day Lost

"Sometimes it's good to be old."

- Anonymous -

My least favourite holiday as a child was Labour Day. It was the last day of freedom, the last bastion of liberty before the inevitable return of incarceration. It was the day that every parent on Sylvan Avenue relished and the one day that every child loathed.

When I was nine, Labour Day was tantamount to a day of national mourning. Instead of squeezing the last joyful moments out of summer by playing baseball or hide and seek, the boys on my street sat sadly on the curb. All day long we lamented, ashen-faced and despondent because school arrived the next day.

"Maybe it's a mistake." Billy said wistfully.

"No, my mom says we have to go back tomorrow." I replied sadly.

"Maybe there'll be a war," Charlie suggested hopefully.

"I wish," Roy said flatly.

"My brother says that some children in Africa don't have schools. He's says they're illiterate," I added.

"Lucky!"

"Yeah, they sure are."

"He also says they have something called famines. So they don't have to eat vegetables either."

"Double lucky!"

"I hate vegetables."

"Me too."

The conversation would peter out until an adult passed by: "School starts tomorrow kids! Are you looking forward to it?" Then they'd start to laugh. Every adult on the street would ask us the same disingenuous question. And then came that inevitable ominous laugh. Sometimes it's good to be old.

After the adults moved along, there'd be long silences punctuated by deep sighs reminiscent of the lamentations of disembodied spirits or soap opera actors.

Later that afternoon Glynnis Jones strutted by. She was ten and entering grade six.

"So you boneheads start grade five tomorrow. Good luck. You'll need it."

"Why?"

"Only the best students pass grade five. And the best students are girls."

"That's not true!"

"My mother says I'm singular," Glynnis boasted.

"Does that mean you can't get a date?" I asked.

All the guys laughed.

"No, you moron. It means girls are unique. My mother read it in *The Female Unique* by Germaine Greer. It says girls can do anything boys can do – only better!"

"Not football."

"Oh really? Then why are the best football players women?"

"Name one!"

"Fran Tarkenton."

"He's a guy!"

"Then why is her name, Fran? And what about Rosie Grier? You can't tell me that she's a guy!"

"Do you boys even know that Labour Day is for girls?"

"How do you figure?

"Well, women have babies, don't they? And when they have a baby it's called labour, isn't it? So today is girls' day."

"But my dad says Labour Day is for unions."

"Where do you think babies come from, ignoramus?"

I thought they came from the pumpkin patch (still do) but decided not to make an issue of it.

Labour day came and went, Glynnis Jones not withstanding. And each passing Labour Day found Billy, Roy, Charlie and I sitting gloomily on the curb until I moved away at age sixteen.

Next Labour Day, I'd like to drive by Sylvan Avenue for old times' sake. I wouldn't be surprised to see Billy, Roy and Charlie still sitting on the curb crying the blues. But wherever I am I'll always vividly remember the sadness of Labour Days past. And when I pass morose children lamenting the end of summer, what do I do?

I say, "School starts tomorrow kids! Are you looking forward to it?" And then I laugh. Oh boy do I laugh…

Sometimes it's good to be old.

Valentine's Day Is For The Birds

*"For this was sent on Seynt Valentyne's day
Whan every foul cometh ther to choose his mate."*
~ Chaucer ~

Valentine's Day isn't my favourite holiday either. It is strewn with romantic misadventures and unrealized expectations. When I was eight, it was the day that separated the popular kids from the also-rans. I remember making cardboard mailboxes in art class so we could all 'mail' our valentines on February 14th. That's how we found out who liked us and who didn't.

I got two valentines that year- one from Jill (who sent valentines to every boy in class) and the other from my teacher (who obviously felt sorry for me.) I still refer to it as the Valentine's Day Massacre.

Years later when I was a nerdy teenager, I met Jennifer. Tall, skinny and awkward, I tried my best to be cool but Jennifer was infinitely cooler. She was worldly and she loved to tease me…

"Oh Ray," she'd say with sincere insincerity. "You're as handsome as Robert Redford."

"Really?"

"Psyche!"

Despite her ribbing, I was desperately in love with her.

"Be my Valentine, Jennifer? I'll take you out for a fancy dinner. I'll be really deboner.

"Deboner?" she laughed. "Isn't that a guy who guts fish?" The word you're looking for is 'debonair.'

I must admit I'm not very debonair or French. So, one day when she unexpectedly kissed me in the French style, I was totally shocked. She laughed at my reaction. I was bewildered to say the least. Only years later did I think of a comeback line: "Pardon me, madam, but I believe your tongue is in my cheek."

At university, I once went to a Valentine's Day party with my brother Jay. Within minutes, several young women were sitting in a circle around him while he told stories about his drag racing adventures. I bet if he'd said his name was "Bond, James Bond," they'd have believed it.

I said hello to the hostess who irritably replied, "Oh, why can't you be more like your brother? He's so handsome."

Dazed, I apologized and started cleaning up the dishes for her. All I needed was an apron.

As Jay said later, "Ray you're going to make some woman a great wife someday."

Although I'm still single, I'd never really given up on Valentine's Day. At least not until last year when I dropped by the department store to return some pants. There was a beautiful woman at the counter. She gave me a smile. It was obvious we were connecting! Then she made her move:

"Could I have your telephone number?" she asked

demurely.

I gave her a wink.

"Please, I really need your phone number!"

"You must think I'm pretty cute," I said with a swagger, winking at her co-worker.

"Well, err...actually."

"No need to say it," I gushed. "It'll be our little secret."

When she handed me my refund and I knew it was love!

I almost asked her out for Valentine's Day then and there except for another customer standing behind me. He was an eighty year-old man returning a tie.

I was waiting for her to expedite matters when unexpectedly she smiled at him demurely and said, "Could I have your phone number?"

"Why do you want my phone number?" he asked.

"Because it's store policy not to give a refund without it."

Her co-worker looked at me and began to snicker. Suddenly aware of the situation, I thought it best to leave. She was obviously making fun of the old man's choice in ties. Poor fashion sense is such a tragedy!

Although I'm still looking for love, I've pretty much given up on Valentine's Day. I guess Chaucer was right. 'For this was sent on Seynt Valentyne's day. Whan every foul cometh ther to choose his mate.' Translated into plain English it means Valentine's Day is for the birds.

I concur.

A Moving Christmas

"At Christmas, all roads lead home."
~ Marjorie Holmes ~

My brother Jay loves Christmas. He loves the lights, the carols and especially the Christmas trees. At Christmas, he's like a little kid.

When Jay and I bought a house together one fall we weren't thinking about Christmas. Unfortunately, the required renovations left very little room for our prized possessions. We soon found ourselves with three storage units plus a fourth unit back in Alberta where we used to live. Surrounded by tools instead of furniture, a normal Christmas seemed out of the question.

Still, a few weeks later, and despite a house in utter chaos, Jay promised that he'd have everything ready in time for an old-fashioned Christmas. One afternoon, I arrived home to find two huge boxes in middle of the living room next to a pile of two-by-fours and plumbing supplies.

"Look," Jay exclaimed exuberantly. "I've got the Christmas tree out of storage. I said we were going to have an old fashioned Christmas and by gosh so we will!" Jay opened a large box and produced the bottom half of the stunning spruce tree he bought in 2003. He then opened the other container and out came the top half. Unfortunately, it was the pitiful pine he bought in 1997.

Jay looked at it dumfounded.

I couldn't resist having a little fun. "Now there's an old fashioned tree - half spruce and half pine. Oh when will those evil geneticists stop fooling around with Mother Nature?"

"Very funny."

"Maybe we can attach the bottom of the spruce to the top of the pine. Gee, what would you call that, Jay? A pruce or a sprine?"

"The connecting pieces aren't the same size. It won't fit together anyway."

"Well then, how about we attach them with duct tape. That way it'll be a Red Green tree."

"Hilarious," he replied flatly." Right now I feel like throwing it out into the backyard."

"Don't do it," I intoned seriously, "then it'd be a pine in the grass."

"Shut up."

"Look, let's just keep the bottom half of the spruce and decorate it. Then we can sing Christmas carols. "Oh Christmas twig, Oh Christmas twig, we wish you had some branches."

"I told you to shut up!"

"Well at least it'll be easy to put a star on top."

"Enough already."

"Okay, okay. Let's just decorate it. By the way, where are the decorations?"

"Shut up!"

"You're not going to tell me that our Christmas decorations are in the back of the storage unit? It'll take hours to get them out."

"No."

"Where are they, then?

"Muddabumph."

"You're mumbling."

"Muddabumph."

"And by muddabumph, you don't mean they're eight-hundred miles away in Alberta, do you?"

"Shut up!"

The next day, tired of my teasing, Jay suggested that I go visit Mom while he put up the Christmas lights.

"You found the strings? I thought they were lost in storage."

"Nope, I found them. And then I bought all new light bulbs. You wait 'till tonight. You'll be able to see this house from space!"

I returned around seven but there weren't any Christmas lights. Jay was cooking dinner.

"Didn't have time to put up the lights?"

"The strings are up and ready to go."

"Great! Let's have a look."

"I'm cooking."

"That's okay. I'll help. Turn 'em on."

"Muddabumph."

"I can't hear you, you're mumbling again."

"The new light bulbs didn't fit," he answered sheepishly.

I don't get opportunities like that every day so I sprinted outside and pretended to admire the house.

"My goodness but isn't this place impressive? It should be on the Christmas light tour. Why, I bet you could see it from Venus. Hope the glare doesn't disturb the neighbours."

"Oh shut up."

"Never mind, I'm just kidding. I'll put on a Christmas album. How about Holiday for Strings?"

"Very funny!"

"Speaking of Christmas music. Just where is the stereo?"

"Muddabumph."

"By muddabumph do you mean it's in storage too?"

"Muddabumph."

"Never mind, I can guess where it is. How about I sing White Christmas for you instead? It'll bring tears to your eyes."

"Finally, something we can both agree on," Jay smiled.

"Muddabumph." I replied. "Muddabumph."

That year our Christmas was wedged between boxes and brad nailers; presents and power tools. And even though we had half a Christmas tree and no lights, I wouldn't have chosen anyplace else. Because "at Christmas, all roads lead home."

CHAPTER TWELVE:

HELLO, GOODBYE

"Scan Not a Friend With Microscopic Glass
You know his faults, now let his foibles pass.
Life is one long mystery my friend
Live on, live on, the answer's at the end."
~ George Harrison ~

As Evening Falls

"To be absent from the body, is to be present with the
Lord."
~ 2 Corinthians 5:8 ~

Easter didn't mean much to me when I was young. Oh sure, I liked getting chocolate and four days off school, but its spiritual significance was lost on me. In fact when I was little, I was materialistic to a fault. That is until I was ten.

That year my friends and I got to bragging about all the candy we were going to get for Easter. It became quite a competition – each of us ratcheting up the bidding until we were sure that a dozen chocolate rabbits was well within the realm of possibility...It wasn't.

On Easter Sunday all I got was one small chocolate bunny and three miniature candy eggs. The paucity of treats had more to do with my recent dental checkup than any stinginess on Mom and Dad's part, but I felt hard done by as I dejectedly wandered outside. I was hoping to avoid my friends but Barry spotted me from down the street and waived me over. He seemed enormously pleased with himself. When I walked into his living room, I knew why. There were at least thirty large chocolate bunnies as well as numerous baskets of Cadbury Easter cream eggs and other treats. I was so envious I could spit.

"You only got one bunny? That's pathetic!" he sneered condescendingly.

I couldn't think of a reply.

Just then his mother came in puffing on a cigarette and complaining about her "$&#@% kids!" She gave me a derisive glance asking, "What are you doing here?" Then she continued denigrating her children's avarice in the saltiest possible terms. Barry stared out of the window; his bravado quietly slipping away. As I crept out the front door and down the walk, the sound of her profanity-laced diatribe rang in my ears.

When I got home Mom was in the kitchen. "Lunch is almost ready," she smiled. I looked at her gratefully for a long time.

"Thanks for the Easter candy, Mom."

She looked surprised. "You're welcome, sweetie."

Spirituality isn't usually a top of mind subject for the young. The material world is paramount and gratitude is just an archaic word. But as I got older, I began to sense its significance. So I embarked on a spiritual quest of sorts reading a wide variety of books about philosophy and humanism. But it was the New Testament that took me by surprise:

As previously mentioned, in Luke Chapter 15 Christ tells the story of a young man who leaves home with his inheritance and wastes it all on prostitutes and partying. When he comes to his senses, he knows there's no way his father can forgive him. But he heads home anyway, hoping to get a job as a hired hand. Expecting an earful, the boy recites the lines he's practiced over and over again, "Father I have sinned against heaven and you. I'm no longer worthy of being your son." Oddly enough his father ignores the apology. There is no rancor or blame. No I told you so - just forgiveness and gratitude for his son's safe return. I expect it's that way with our Heavenly Father too. When we ask for forgiveness, there is no punishment or rancor or blame. Just absolution. And gratitude that one of his children has come home.

Recently one of my elderly friends passed away. Although her passing was difficult, it was nonetheless dignified and serene. One afternoon near the end, some of her roommates were commiserating outside her door when the topic of the afterlife came up.

Everyone began offering his or her opinions on what dying was like. Asked what I believed, I replied, "I think death is like children playing outside as evening falls. Just as parents call their children home for dinner, God calls each of us - one by one. Some are summoned early and wish they could play a little longer. Some see their friends going home before them and the night becomes lonely and still. But when it's time to enter God's home, there is no sadness – just love and gratitude and forgiveness.

On Good Fridays, I'm grateful for a host of things: family, friends and a Heavenly Father who sent his son to die on a cross for our sins and to prepare an eternal home for us.

"To be absent from the body, is to be present with the Lord."

A comforting thought – especially at Easter.

The Twist of the Tale

Fate gives us the hand, and we play the cards.
~ Arthur Schopenhauer ~

Are we agents of free will or are the currents of our lives preordained? Is life just an aimless series of unrelated events? Or are our experiences part of a greater, fixed plan? Since biblical times there have been numerous accounts of uncannily accurate prophecies:

Moses prophesied the death of Pharaoh's first-born son unless Pharaoh released the Jewish people from their slavery. Pharaoh refused. The next morning Pharaoh's son was dead just as Moses had predicted. But what if Pharaoh had listened?

King Saul begged the prophet Samuel to predict his fate. Samuel, who had repeatedly told the king to abdicate, replied that Saul would die on the battlefield the very next day. Saul stubbornly ignored the warning and was killed along with his sons. But what if he'd relinquished the throne?

Fast-forward to the 19th century and the strange case of Abraham. Abraham was a tall, gangly small town lawyer and politician. He wasn't particularly successful but one day he had an unlikely vision. In the vision he saw himself becoming president. And, in 1860, Abraham Lincoln was indeed elected the sixteenth president of the United States. A few years later, he had another vision, one far more dark and disturbing:

" I retired very late. I had been up waiting for important dispatches from the front. I could not have been long in bed when I fell into a slumber, for I was weary. I soon began to dream. There seemed to be a death-like stillness about me. Then I heard subdued sobs, as if a number of people were weeping. I thought I left my bed and wandered downstairs... I was puzzled and alarmed... I kept on until I arrived at the East Room, which I entered. There I met with a sickening surprise. Before me was a catafalque, on which rested a corpse wrapped in funeral vestments. Around it were stationed soldiers who were acting as guards; and there was a throng of people, gazing mournfully upon the corpse, whose face was covered, others weeping pitifully. 'Who is dead in the White House?' I demanded of one of the soldiers, 'The President,' was his answer; 'he was killed by an assassin.'" (*Recollections of Abraham Lincoln 1847-1865* by Ward Hill Lamon pp.116-117)

According to Lamon, Lincoln refused to believe that the dream pertained to him. He insisted it must be about some other president in some future time. A few days later he was assassinated at Ford's theatre. But what if he'd stayed home that night?

Fast forward again to the 20th century and consider the case of Martin. A Baptist preacher, Martin Luther King Jr. led the equal rights movement despite constant death threats. He too had a vision:

"We've got some difficult days ahead. But it doesn't matter with me now. Because I have been to the mountaintop. And I don't mind. Like anybody, I would like to live a long life. Longevity has its place. But I'm not concerned about that now. I just want to do God's will. And He's allowed me to go up to the mountain. And I've looked over. And I've seen the Promised Land. I may not get there with you. But I want you to know tonight, that we, as a people will get to the Promised Land. And I'm not fearing any man. Mine eyes have seen the glory of the coming of the Lord"

King knew the threats were real but refused to be cowed by them or even by his own dark premonitions of death. The next day he was assassinated on a hotel balcony. But what if he'd chosen the safer course and stayed inside?

Finally, let us look at the case of Winston:

He was one of the giants of the 20th century. He was charismatic, articulate and prolific. His books were best sellers not only in his native England but throughout the world. Even the drawings and paintings he created while relaxing were highly sought after. Despite his compassion, his political activism could divide; even enrage others. He was often vilified and hero-worshipped within the same household.

Winston was keenly aware of the threat caused by his celebrity. In fact, while still a young man, he too had experienced premonitions of his own violent death. Unlike the aforementioned leaders, Winston chose to reduce the risk by entering a self-imposed semi-retirement and by emphasizing humour over strident confrontation. In his last interview he said,

"That's part of our policy …we are humorous and we stand a better chance under that guise, because all the serious people, like Martin Luther King, and Kennedy, and Gandhi, got shot."

And therein lies the twist of the tale. A few days later, John 'Winston' Lennon was shot to death outside his apartment in New York City. His humorous guise had made no difference.

So the question remains, are we agents of destiny or of chance? And how can prophecies come true unless the events of our lives are preordained?

"Fate gives us the cards and we play the hand." Was Schopenhauer right? Consider Abraham, Martin and John and draw your own conclusions.

Maxwell's House

"A dog is the only thing on earth that loves you more than you love yourself."
~ Josh Billings ~

In 1946, the war was over but times were tough in Europe. High unemployment and food shortages were commonplace and crime was ubiquitous.

In order to provide for his family, Dad had little choice but to re-join the military. Worried about Mom and my sisters, he decided to buy a dog to protect them. So he asked one of his buddies where he could get a guard dog.

"I know of a dog. Bred for police work. An eighty-pound Bouvier named Max. But he's a vicious one Hank. Even the cops don't want him.

"Is he a good watch dog?"

"Tough as nails. Never mollycoddled. Though I'm not sure I'd want him around my wife and girls if I were you."

"It's okay, we'll keep him outside."

So that afternoon Dad bought a police dog. On the way home he rehearsed his speech:

"Now remember children this isn't a pet. So don't try to touch him or make any sudden moves."

Mom saw them coming. It was love at first sight. She ran outside and before Dad could stop her, she fell on her knees and hugged that vicious, unpredictable dog.

Dad was momentarily mesmerized. Then he shouted, "Are you crazy, Marsha? Max is a killer!"

But as Mom hugged him, Max also seemed transfixed. Mom's embrace was the first kindness Max had ever received. Soon he began to whimper. Then he put his muzzle in Mom's hand. It was clear Mom wasn't the only one smitten by love at first sight that day.

Soon after, Dad was sent on a training mission. When he came back, Max met him with tail wagging. Dad gave him a pat on the head, hugged and kissed the children and made a beeline for Mom. As Dad leaned over to give Mom a kiss, he heard a low growl. He tried again. This time he was met with barking and snarling teeth. Dad ruefully backed away. Mom had become disputed territory. This was now Maxwell's house.

Max took his duties seriously. He doted on the children, walking them to and from school. In between times, Mom and Max would sit in the garden. Mom would read, and Max would lie down contentedly at her feet. Sometimes Mom would hear a noise.

"Max, is someone at the door?"

Max would obediently get up and check. A short series of woofs would alert her to a visitor. Otherwise he'd return stiff-legged and drop at her feet with a resounding thud and a sigh. His love for Mom notwithstanding, Max didn't like fool's errands.

Although he was a fine protector, Max was far from perfect. Any careless cat entering the yard could have told you that. And, like many French dogs, he was wont to "cherchez les femmes." Every night Max would slip away in the darkness to find romance- much to my father's annoyance. The next morning there'd be a single "woof" outside the door. If Max heard Dad's angry footstep, he'd hide out in the back yard. If Mom opened the door, he'd be waiting patiently. Then, head cocked to one side, he'd listen as she lectured him on his wanton lifestyle. The sermon concluded; he'd trot inside for breakfast.

One afternoon in the summer of 1951, Dad took Mom out to the lake.

"What's wrong with you?" he asked. "You're not smiling."

Mom replied, "I don't know. I feel like I just lost my best friend."

When they arrived home Max was missing. A neighbour said he'd heard gunfire. Dad went out to search. A few hours later, he found Max's body dumped in a nearby farmer's field. He'd been shot. When Dad returned home, Mom said quietly, "You don't have to tell me, I already know."

The events of that day remain shrouded in mystery. Many neighbouring homes had been broken into but not Mom and Dad's. Had someone tried to rob the house and been confronted by an angry Bouvier? Everyone in town knew that Max would have taken a bullet for my mom. Sadly, it may have been his final act of love for her.

They say, "A dog is the only thing on earth that loves you more than you love yourself." And I believe it too. Because that's the way it was - at Maxwell's house.

Goodbye Henry

The heart is not judged by how much you love,
but by how much you are loved by others.
~ L. Frank Baum ~

What is the measure of a life? By North American standards it is wealth, power and fame. And without question, the media lionize the renowned in death based solely on their celebrity. But by what yardstick should we measure a life?

Henry Kuiper was born on September 11, 1920 in the Netherlands. He married his first wife Corrie after the war and had six wonderful children. He wasn't famous. He wasn't rich. He worked in a factory. And every day he put his dreams of being a sea captain and sailing the ocean aside in order to provide for his family. He was a devoted father and soft-spoken to a fault.

Although happy in Holland, he moved his family to Canada in 1960 so that his children would have better economic opportunities than he did. He settled in Guelph, a long way from the ocean he loved. And he started over. When his first wife Corrie died in 1978, he took it hard but didn't complain. He pushed on because there was still a family who needed him.

In 1979, he met my mother and they married the next year. I wasn't quite sure what to make of Henry. For many years we had a cordial if distant relationship. I found his quiet demeanor a little unnerving and he wasn't sure what to make of my constant joke telling. That all changed in 1993:

One early spring afternoon Henry went blind. In his inimitable way he announced it quietly, "I can't see."

I would have come unglued but he was the very soul of composure. The doctor later explained that the blood vessels in his eyes had burst filling the area with blood. His only hope was that the blood could be removed surgically and that the retinas were not damaged.

Over the next several months, I took him on the six-hour return trip to an ophthalmologist in Calgary numerous times. It was during those trips that we really got to know each other. He learned to laugh at my corny jokes and I learned to appreciate the silences that good friends share. A couple of days before his birthday, I asked him if he had a birthday wish.

"To see," he replied simply.

The next day the hospital called unexpectedly. Henry's surgery was scheduled for the next day: September 11th. Coincidentally, it was his birthday. Thankfully, the surgery was a complete success and Henry could see again.

By 1999, Henry was in very poor health. We moved back to Vancouver Island, settling in Parksville so he could enjoy his ocean. I was lucky enough to be one of his caregivers. Several times a week, we went to Rathtrevor Park or Parksville Beach and then for coffee. I loved those outings.

The final one came when he was living at a local lodge, a wonderful facility with caring and compassionate staff. A few days before Christmas, we went to A&W for coffee and ice cream as we had scores of times before. The server handed him the biggest ice cream cone I'd ever seen. He beamed like a little kid! And despite the ravages of heart failure, he ate the entire thing. A few days later the nursing staff explained that he was now to ill for our daily trips.

Just after eight PM on New Year's Day, the on-duty nurse at the facility called to say that Henry wanted to see me. He was on morphine and could barely move but he didn't complain. I told him how much we all loved him. And as I was leaving he threw his hand over the bed railing.

"He wants to shake hands, goodbye," the nurse explained quietly.

It must have taken an enormous physical effort but it was so like him. He passed away the next morning.

"The heart is not judged by how much you love, but by how much you are loved by others."

Goodbye Henry. You were loved and then some.

THANKSGIVING MEMORIES

*"The true measure of a man is how he treats someone
who can do him absolutely no good."*
~ Attributed to Ann Landers ~

When I was a child, I looked forward to Thanksgiving. It was a time for turkey dinners and pumpkin pie and an extra day off school, but more importantly it was a chance to spend some time with my brother-in-law Vic.

Every family has its Thanksgiving traditions. Ours involved driving north to close up the cottage for the winter. Vic was the undisputed star of our weekends at the cottage. He was a natural born comedian. Short and thin, he bore more than a passing resemblance to Bing Crosby. And like Bing, he had an easygoing style that endeared him to everyone who knew him. Vic was the funniest man I ever met but his happy-go-lucky nature belied a deeply serious side. For Vic was also a profoundly religious man: his love of humour only exceeded by his love of God.

My father was born into a poor family. He learned early in life that the only way out of abject poverty is through hard work. So he was relentless in his resolve that his children learn the value of hard work too. He found Vic's easy-going attitude perplexing. He also thought that his son-in-law should be working at the cottage, not relaxing.

One afternoon he sent us out to the lake to clean up the boat slip.

"Go do a man's work," he exclaimed glaring at my brother-in-law.

We dutifully hopped into the water and began removing armfuls of disgusting, smelly weeds. After about twenty minutes Vic whispered, "Look over here, Ray."

I glanced over and started to laugh.

He had deposited an armful of weeds on his chest, which looked for all the world like a humongous bush of green hair. Smiling, he declared, "Now who says I'm not a man!"

Given the paucity of space at the cottage, my brother Jay and I were often reduced to sleeping on the living room floor while Vic and my sister Thea slept in the tiny bedroom nearby. One night, after lights out, all was quiet until we heard Vic whispering with mock gravity, "Stop it, Thea!" After a few minutes went by, he added in an exaggerated whisper, "No, Thea, I'm not in the mood, tonight. I have a headache. Shh, Thea, be quiet or the boys will hear!"

Naturally, he knew all the while that the boys were listening intently. His feigned romantic reluctance brought such a cacophony of laughter that Dad had to get out of bed to put an end to the shenanigans.

Although, I'm sure Vic would rather have been playing golf, he always spent time with me at the cottage. We often played Scrabble or Monopoly and even as a child I appreciated his kindness. I used to ask Vic all of the questions that a young boy is afraid to ask his father: questions about life and feelings and girls. And he wasn't the least bit squeamish about giving me honest and direct answers.

So when I asked him about his belief in Christianity, he was as straightforward as ever. He quoted me John 3:16 "For God so loved the world, that he gave his only begotten son, that whosoever believeth in Him, should not perish, but have everlasting life." He helped me understand that God had a special plan for every human life and when we ask Christ into our hearts, that plan is put in motion. And he noted that Christ's sacrifice on the cross was an act of pure kindness because we can never repay it.

Each year as Thanksgiving approaches I am reminded me of those halcyon days at the lake. My Dad is gone now. But I'm thankful that he taught me the value of hard work and self-reliance. Vic is gone too. But I'm thankful that he led me to a reassuring faith as well as a healthy respect for the lighter side of life.

"The true measure of a man is how he treats someone who can do him absolutely no good."

Words worth considering.

11548420R00116